A LATINA'S (

MW00441725

A LATINA'S GUIDE TO MONEY

Eva Macias

Printed in the United States of America
ISBN-13: 978-0-692-07292-9

DEDICATION

This book is dedicated to my parents, my family, my friends, my clients, and my husband...who always support and encourage me to work toward my DREAMS.

But most importantly, I want to thank GOD for choosing me to deliver this vision of impacting millions of lives through my journey called life.

TABLE OF CONTENTS

Want to get started right away?
Visit www.EvaMacias.com/60min to create your
60-minute financial plan for the future.

INTRODUCTION

I grew up in a Latin family, and the two things I don't remember ever hearing anyone talk about were sex and money.

In this book, we're going to talk about money.

When I was beginning to make a good income, I knew it wasn't going to last forever. I wanted to take advantage of that money while I still could. So, I decided to set up my own 401(k) because I didn't have one through my employer at the time. But the whole process proved to be very confusing and overwhelming.

Then I reached out to my older sisters to ask what financial plans they had, but they were as confused about it as I was. Then I attended a workshop, and one of the speakers said, "You will most likely have the same retirement plan as your parents." I didn't know what retirement plan my parents had, so I asked my mom, and all she said was, "Social Security."

My parents were living on a retirement check that was less than my current car payment.

I became upset. Really upset. I knew my mom worked hard all her life to provide for our family. How could it be that she made so little? I thought, "How come nobody ever told me this? How come people don't know about this? Why don't they care?!"

After looking at my parents' situation from all possible angles, asking fervent questions, and dealing with my own underlying anger and upset, I soon recognized it was not that people didn't care. It was that any and all available financial information was overwhelming and unfamiliar to my Latin community, and my friends and family didn't know who they could trust. The 2008 financial crisis had been so terrible. Fear was rampant in every household, including mine.

I had $10K monthly living expenses. My credit card debt was more than $100,000. I almost lost my house *and* my car (the one that cost more each month than my parents' retirement checks). Creditors were calling all day, every day. I received threats of lawsuits. My many sleepless nights were filled with sadness, depression, and incessant negative thoughts of worry and anxiety.

And then it hit me. I was headed in the same direction as my parents. I saw the impact of their financial decisions as well as my own. I didn't know anything about the system and neither did my parents. Possibilities were endless for them. But they didn't know. And, because they didn't know, they are now living the consequences.

I didn't want to live those consequences.

But I had been thinking and acting like I'd be young forever. I spent my early twenties shopping and spending. And while I was going through a financial mess, I was also trying to save someone else (my boyfriend at the time). Even though we all hear sayings like, "fill up your cup first or put on your oxygen mask first," my money was funding someone else's priorities, not mine. So, I was squandering my future and well-being because I was doing all that shopping and spending and rescuing.

I kept droning to myself, "I am a smart woman. Why is this happening to me?" But what I should have been asking was, "How come I *allowed* this to happen to me?"

So instead of continuing to complain about the situation, I did something to fix it instead. It became my priority to get out of the financial quagmire I was in. I started paying attention to my money. I was determined to learn the system. I became responsible for my money. I worked and studied and tested to receive my "Life Agent" license with the State of California. Eva and Associates would not exist if I hadn't paid attention to how retirement was for my parents.

In the process of learning all I could, I came across women who didn't make a lot of money, but still spent a lot more, and they wondered, "Where did my money go?" And I'm thinking, "It's not that it's going anywhere, you just don't bring in enough according to your responsibility." Those things that happen in our everyday lives, whether it's shopping or eating out or spending more than we make, have become automatic. I noticed that we are just too busy to notice.

I also noticed that sometimes we take on the perceptions of other people. If you hang out with the same group of people all the time, their opinions and behaviors become a little numb to you. This is very common among the Latin culture in general as well as Latinas in particular.

And one way that manifested in the Latin culture is called the *cundinas*. It's a very special financial commitment, and it's been around in my culture for ages. Even today, my best friend practices this often.

It's a 12-week program where a group of people (let's say, 12) commit to saving a certain amount of money each week (let's say, $100), and they each give their $100 to someone they may not even know, who is then trusted to distribute the $1,200 according to the tenets of the *cundinas*. So, they are trusting that this person is going to be someone who will take the $1,200 and give it to the next person in the *cundinas* the following week.

So, the first person gets the $1,200, then the next week's $1,200 goes to the second person, the next to the third person, and so on each week for 12 weeks. The 12th person receives the final $1,200, and the program is over. In effect, it is a 12-week savings program where you're trusting that everyone will keep their word, and eventually you'll receive your $1,200 share.

It's the mindset behind it which is fascinating to me. Each person is willing to give away their money in the hope that it will come back. But I think, if you've already built the weekly savings habit by being in the *cundinas* for 12 weeks, why not continue with the same good habit and put it in a bank account that has your name on it instead? That way, you watch it grow and have access to it, instead of waiting for it to come back.

The answer most Latina clients and friends give, in one way or another, is that it is too hard. I 100% believe the reason is because nobody is holding you accountable. The *cundinas* holds you accountable to put in the $100. So, you do it, because you don't want to look stupid. You don't want to feel like you don't have it. Whatever ego conversations come up for you, you're going to make sure you contribute that $100 a week.

But a bank does not do that. It is your responsibility to do it. You are accountable to yourself.

I think as Latinas we chatter this fear and think, "We just have to do it. We're going to do it." But when it comes to giving it to yourself, you don't put in the same effort. You silence your fears with excuses. So, it's interesting to see how, when faced with being accountable to the *cundinas,* we're able to give our money to someone else. But we don't do the same thing for ourselves.

Unfortunately, nobody discusses all of the emotions we hold back about money because we're so fucking scared. We are afraid that, if we express them, we're going to look vulnerable or weak or embarrassed or whatever it is. But, guess what? I've felt that, too. Only now I've learned that's where I hold my power...it's in the awareness of my vulnerability and my awareness of letting those emotions show up.

And then I follow my financial plan anyway.

I've done several podcasts discussing financial planning for different audiences, and a key thing I've noticed that comes up often for me is that money is a result. It is the result of the consistency of your actions—actions taken or not taken.

And the result you see manifests in the form of your account balances...*today and tomorrow.* What do your account balances say about the consistency of your actions?

My hope is that this book gives women an opportunity to get honest with themselves about their money in order to create a sustainable financial plan that funds their priorities and provides peace of mind. Consistent actions can lead any woman to the life of her dreams…including you.

Chapter One

GET REAL WITH YOUR FINANCIAL SITUATION

*Understand that 'I want and I wish' versus
'I will and I'm committed' are very different mindsets.*

When clients sit down with me for their first appointment, I ask, "How much is your net income?" And the answer for women is most often, "I have no idea." That immediately tells me that they're not paying attention to the money that's coming in, but even worse is they're probably not paying attention to the money that's going out.

This was certainly true for me.

I just wanted to know, how much money was deposited into my bank account? That was my biggest concern. Questions such as...Am I bringing in enough money? What's the difference between gross and net income? And How much money do I owe? did not even occur to me to ask.

In fact, there were many times, usually on Mondays after a weekend of mindless spending, where I wondered how much money was in my bank account. Problem is, I didn't want to find out. My fear of "not enough" caused me to not pay attention. Because, if I didn't look at it, it would go away, right?

Not a chance.

It didn't go away until I started to look at my finances and ask myself some serious questions, such as: "Why am I spending that kind of money there? What are my financial priorities? Am I funding what's important to me? How much do I owe? How long until I retire?"

These are now just a few of the questions I ask clients every day.

Many times, clients know how much money is coming in, but they have no idea how their spending reflects their priorities. Most people have debt. So, when I ask, "Is spending your priority?" the answer is usually "Of course not!" That's when I must point out that, "Your finances say otherwise."

That's a big aha moment for women, and that's when they become willing to pay attention and start getting real with what's going on in their lives.

And so, our discussion begins. And I dive deep into your finances, your priorities, and your life experiences with questions like:

- How much money do you make?
- How old are you?
- Are you married or single?
- How many children do you have or do you want to have?
- What are your three main goals?
- What are your basic expenses?
- How much do you save and in what accounts?
- When do you want to retire?
- What does your retirement look like?

I ask these personal questions so I can determine what to recommend based on where you are and where you want to be. And now it's your turn to ask yourself the following questions so you can get real with your financial situation and have whatever that conversation looks like for you.

Maybe you're $30,000 in debt, but only make minimum payments. Maybe you say you want abundance, yet you're willing to spend money on a designer purse. Maybe you're a mom who enjoys buying things for your children, but you're emotionally spending on things for yourself, too?

It's time to get honest with yourself. Where are you financially? Are you spending in a way that aligns with your goals and values? The following questions will help you figure that out.

HOW OFTEN DO YOU *THINK* ABOUT MONEY INSTEAD OF *PLAN* ABOUT MONEY WITH AN ACTUAL BUDGET?

People always want to improve their financial situation. They have endless conversations about money. They stress out about money. They waste their time and mental energy because they ruminate about money woes rather than create a workable and easy-to-follow solution.

Stop thinking and start planning. If you're married, your spouse needs to know what's going on, too. Ladies, how often do we hide our spending habits? Do you have a secret Macy's card that you haven't told him about? Get your spouses involved in your monthly budget. If there are two separate incomes coming in, it's especially important that both of you know what money is going out. Instead of talking about money or being stressed out about money, you and your partner need to filter that energy into asking, "What do we need to do in this moment to support our goals? Let's set aside time to figure this out." (And if you run into resistance about that, see Chapter 8: Communicating About Money With Your Partner.)

WHAT ARE YOUR FINANCIAL GOALS?

Some people have gone through life without giving much thought to what their financial goals might be. Something big often must happen—a life-changing event that serves as a wake-up call and impacts them in a financial way—before they start setting goals. Don't wait for that to happen. Take the time to sit down and figure out what your financial goals are.

What are you planning to do with all the money you've been earning on a monthly or bi-weekly basis? What are some of the big things that you want to do before you die? Do you want to travel? Do you want to send your kids to college? Do you want to be a homeowner? Do you want to live comfortably one day? All of these things require thought.

It's important to figure out what tools can ultimately get you where you want to be. What will help you take action and start accomplishing these goals? Write them down. Believe that you can achieve them. Create a plan that will help get you there. When you apply yourself, the end results will show. All the research and planning you did will ultimately pay off.

WHAT IS YOUR NET INCOME?

How much money do you make each month?

First and foremost, it's very important to know how much money you net monthly. Often when I meet with clients, they don't even know how much money they bring in. They guess a number instead of actually looking at and understanding their paycheck. If you simply take the time to look at your paycheck, you'll know the amount of money that's coming in as well as the amount of money that is available to go out. When budgeting, make sure you know the exact difference between your net and your grosses.

How much taxes are taken out of your paycheck?

Women need to understand the difference between the impact of gross versus net. I usually ask clients, "What would you rather do…pay your taxes now or later?" Normally, they say "later." Then I say, "Did you know that by paying later, you can't be sure how much tax you're going to be paying? On the other hand, at this moment, you know exactly how much your tax bracket is. With that in mind, would you rather pay your taxes now or later?" Make sure you understand your paycheck and know what's coming in before taxes (gross) and what's coming in after taxes (net).

HOW MUCH ARE YOUR MONTHLY EXPENSES?

What are your basic monthly expenses?

It's critical to know your monthly expenses. Monthly expenses are the things you can't live without: food, shelter, gas for your car. You need to sort all your bills, including all your utility bills, your credit bills, your rent or mortgage bill, your food expenses, and any bill that you need to pay each month. Too frequently, it is easy to forget autopayments such as gym membership fees or subscriptions to magazines, which can impact the amount you actually need for monthly expenses.

Be aware of every single expense, such as car payments and insurance payments, and even the small things, like treats or entertainment for your kids. If you can say with certainty each month, "I have X amount of expenses," you'll know immediately if the money you have coming in can support your monthly expenses.

How much are you spending on food?

For most of my clients, food is the number one expense that needs to be controlled. It's critical to determine how much you're spending on groceries and how much you're spending on take-out or dining. I often get families who will say something like, "We spent about $600 on groceries and $500 on eating out this month." But when I ask them to give me their bank statement, the numbers don't match up.

Instead, they're actually spending $1,200 on groceries and $800 on eating out! You need to set a budget for groceries as well as eating out, and then stick to it. I know it's much easier to say, "You know what, I'm not cooking today, let's just go eat out," or "I'm feeling lazy tonight," or "I got out of work a little bit late." And then your food expenses go up.

Everyone has a different budget when it comes to groceries and dining out. That's normal. But you must know your unique family situation and say, "We're only going to use this amount for eating out from now on because feeding a family of six is very expensive when we eat out so often." Set a definite amount of money aside each month for groceries and restaurants, and make sure that amount doesn't interfere with your financial goals.

How much do you spend on entertainment?

It's time to get real. Know how much you spend on entertainment each month. Clients will ask, "Are eating out and going to the movies considered entertainment?" If those activities entertain you, then yes, they are entertainment.

So, ask yourself how often you're doing it and how much it's costing you. Some people will want entertainment two or three times a week. They'll go to movies or comedy shows on a regular basis because they think this is okay. I'm not saying it isn't okay, but make sure you can afford it!

If you've taken care of all your responsibilities and have money left over for fun, that's wonderful. But most people are entertaining first *before* making sure all their financial responsibilities have been met. That's where the stress comes in. And how much fun is entertainment if it leads to financial stress? These days, it's easy to find good entertainment that's free. Look into it! There are many ways to entertain you and your family with very little expense.

How much do you spend on your physical appearance?

Ladies, take note of how much you're spending on maintaining your physical appearance. When I ask, "What are your expenses?" most women never include the amount they spend on physical appearance in their estimates. The truth is, it can get a little pricey. So be honest with yourself and say, "I get my nails done every two weeks. I get my hair done every six to eight weeks. I buy make-up and skin care every month. Occasionally I visit the spa, get massages, get facials."

It's important to know you can have it all—*as long as you budget for it.* I have met many women who spend $300 a month to get their nails done but put nothing toward retirement. Make sure you've taken care of your responsibilities first and know how much you're spending. By all means, don't hesitate to look for discounts, coupons, and special deals!

Do you pay for gym memberships that you don't use?

Some clients forget to add their gym memberships as an expense. When they remember and say, "Oh yeah, I've been a member for five years, but I never go." So, my next question is always, "Why do you keep paying for this membership month after month?" Many of us decide that, because we're renewing the membership each month, we'll start exercising, lose weight, and finally get in shape…but then we still never go. Is that happening to you? If so, get real with yourself and cancel the membership now. Why would you pay for something you're not using? When you're ready to start using it, you can always go back. Sometimes people will argue, "But I pay a very low membership fee." Even so, you're still losing money by paying for something you're not using. Cancel it!

If you *are* using your gym membership, that's wonderful. In many cases, you can even prepay. Costco usually does this with its store memberships. You can prepay for about two to three years, and it becomes much cheaper at the discounted price. It comes to $10 or $12 per month. Know that you don't have to do it the traditional way. There are different companies that help you stay fit, but let you do it at a very low cost.

Are taxes and homeowner's insurance included with your mortgage?

Some people like the responsibility of paying their own taxes and insurance separate from their mortgage; other people prefer to have it included in the same payment. Make sure you know what's true for you. If your taxes and homeowner's insurance aren't included in your mortgage, you've got to make sure you're adding those additional payments to your monthly expenses. If you make those payments twice a year, you can prepare yourself financially prior to those dates by saving the monthly installments. That way, you'll have the money ready. No stress, no mess.

If you delay paying on time, you'll get a penalty and you'll be giving even more money away. Homeowner's insurance comes once a year, and the property tax is twice a year. Prepare yourself in advance so you can handle your homeowner's insurance and taxes responsibly.

Do you know what's considered an emergency expense?

Emergencies can include a faulty alternator, an abscess tooth, four flat tires, a lost job, a broken bone, a visit to the vet, and more. An emergency fund is meant to support you and your family in day-to-day life when such emergencies occur. Of course, you hope these things will never happen, but in case they do, it's best to be prepared.

HOW MUCH DO YOU OWE?

How much credit card or personal debt do you *really* have? What are the interest rates?

When you know the exact total amount that you owe, the amount of minimum payments, the amount of monthly payments you're sending, and the interest rates, you have the foundation to build a plan that can ultimately ensure your financial freedom. The ultimate goal is to be debt-free. I often work with women who say, "Well, I always send more than the minimum payment." That's great, but it's important to understand how these actions are helping you get out of debt.

How much do you owe in student loans?

No matter how much you owe, if you can afford your monthly payment (in other words, you're not requesting a deferral), you need to pay your student loans. If you don't, they will garnish your wages. Remain aware of your current payments and balance, have a system in place for the future, and stop stressing out about your student loans. When you make your payments each month, remember that your education was worth it.

How much do you owe on your car?

Knowing how much you owe on your car can definitely help you get out of debt more quickly. People often prefer low car payments, but if you end up getting into contracts of five to seven years, you're just giving more money away in the long run. When you budget each month, know how much you owe and plan to pay a little bit more than the required amount. Then you can calculate how quickly you'll be able get out of that car debt. As soon as your car is free and clear, that is one less expense for you to worry about.

How much do you owe on your mortgage?

When it comes to your mortgage, just because the word *refinance* exists doesn't mean you have to use it or do it. Most people will say, "I want to pay off my house in 30 years." That's wonderful. It's a great goal to have, but life happens along the way and you may end up refinancing your house...once or even a few times. Every single time you do that, you're delaying how quickly you're going to get out of that mortgage debt.

Know how much you owe and develop a strategy that can ultimately reduce the number of years on which you owe your mortgage. Sending one or two payments more each year toward your principal can go a long way. If you keep your age in mind, you can start doing the math: "After X number of years that I still owe on my mortgage, I will be debt-free by this or that day." That's a great and motivating feeling.

Remember to pay close attention to your mortgage statements because people on the other side sometimes make mistakes. We're all human. It's your responsibility to review your mortgage statement to ensure that all of your payments are being credited appropriately.

How long will it take you to get out of debt?

When you're building a financial plan, you must ask yourself this key question. The most common answers I hear are, "I don't know" or "I don't think I'll ever be out of debt." That's no way to be responsible for your money. Once again, if you are well-informed about your financial situation, you can ultimately create a plan to become debt-free. Know how much you need to send to a credit card in order to set off a domino effect of paying one off so that you can eventually use those funds to pay another one off. If you can create a system that works for you, you'll be able to calculate how many years it will be before you're out of debt.

HOW MUCH DO YOU SAVE?

How many months of reserves do you have in an emergency funds account?

An emergency fund is, as the term implies, for emergencies. This money is set aside for emergency reasons only and must be used for emergency reasons only. On the flipside, I've talked to people who've experienced genuine emergencies, but were afraid to touch this fund because they worried about not having the funds anymore. But that's why you create the fund in the first place, so you can access it at a time of need.

People often ask me, "How many months of reserves am I supposed to have in my emergency funds account?" It's not so much what amount you are *supposed* to have, but what amount gives you peace of mind at the end of the day. I used to say you need to have three to six months' worth, but with the current economy, you should really aim to have a minimum of six months to a year's worth.

It's much harder for people to find a new job these days. You can give yourself and your family a little more financial security if you set aside enough for six months to a year. If you're able to find a new job prior to that running out, all the more power to you.

Are you saving for your kids' college expenses?

Once you have a child, you can start planning for their college expenses two weeks after they're born. Don't wait until they're 18. Parents want the best for their kids, and that includes ensuring that they get a good education. I have many nieces and nephews, and as long as they're going to school, our family will support them. But college tuition can be very expensive over time, and the cost is always going up. So, start early, and know what types of accounts are available for your kids' college expenses and how they work.

WHAT ARE YOU DOING TO FINANCE YOUR RETIREMENT?

How old do you want to be when you retire?

Most people I speak with say that they don't know how old they want to be when they retire or that they never even thought about it. That response always surprises me because I've been thinking about it since I was 27—not because I didn't love what I did, but because I witnessed my parents retire at a relatively early point in their lives with very little money. Having a good idea of when you want to retire will help you ensure that everything is in order financially when you do retire. If you want to stop working at a certain point and you're not saving money for it, you likely won't have enough when you retire.

How much money do you want to retire with on a monthly basis?

Many people also have no idea how much money they want or need to retire. I ask them, "Don't you want to make sure you have your monthly living expenses covered? Every family is different. What does that number look like for you?" They often respond that, considering inflation, they have no idea what that number will be. When I ask them what number they see in their head, some people give me numbers that are more fantasy than reality. When I ask what they're doing to achieve this goal, the answer is often, "nothing."

Whoa. It's time to get real.

No matter your income, you need to start putting a certain percentage of that money away into an account that will support you. That way, whenever you do retire, the money will be there waiting. First figure out how much you want when you retire. Figure out what the big picture looks like. And then work backward. Break your goal down into little chunks so you will feel capable of accomplishing it over time.

How much are you contributing to retirement accounts?

Normally I tell people to put 15% of their income away in a retirement account. You'll often hear a number between 10% and 15% from difference sources. I always like to go with 15%. Clients often ask, "Well, what is everybody else doing?" Don't worry about what everybody else is doing. This is your money and your retirement. Worry about what's going to work for you.

Consider these factors: your age, how much money you're bringing in, and how much you want to receive monthly upon retirement. Knowing these basic numbers will allow you to customize a plan according to your individual needs. It's about what's best for you, your family, and your goals. If you're not putting money into a retirement account that's helping you reach your monthly retirement goal, then it's time to begin.

What if I don't make a lot of money?

At a certain point, it's important to know the amount of money that you're making, regardless of whether it's a little bit or a lot. The important thing is where you are putting your money. If you have a lot of money coming in but aren't investing it wisely, that money could be going anywhere. Even if you aren't making a lot, make a habit of putting portions of it away for the future. Create a situation in which you control your money. Don't let it control you!

It is my hope that you will use these questions to honestly assess your financial situation. It's vital to start paying attention to the things you are doing and what you are spending. Most people are too busy to notice.

But if you start paying attention, elevating yourself, spending time with those who are better off financially (and maybe even better off emotionally), soon you'll be excited and enthusiastic about stepping up your game. And you'll be all the richer for it, in more ways than money.

Chapter Two

KNOWLEDGE IS POWER, BUT ONLY WHEN YOU APPLY IT

Remember that a combination of knowledge, action, confidence, commitment, and faith—all those things together—will get you to the finish line.

When my clients and I have our first appointment, they're required to provide all relevant financial information, including answering lots of personal questions. They give me all their paychecks and bank statements. They list their basic expenses and what they spend on everything. They give me their insurance plans and retirement documents. They discuss their top three goals and why they want them. This is their way of "getting real" by handing it all over to me to discern, make a budget, and provide recommendations.

It's quite eye-opening for them, and sometimes embarrassing, to be so transparent. Many women don't want anyone to know the state of their financial affairs. Many want to keep spending like they always do. When I sit across 20-year-olds, I know where they're coming from and have a good sense of where their money goes. Because I've been there, done that.

I often say, "Okay, I totally get it. You want to have your nails done. You want to drive the nicest car. You want to wear hot clothes, and there's nothing wrong with Louis Vuitton purses. I get it. I totally get it. I was that girl. But wouldn't it be better to have money in the bank instead, so relying on people to praise you because you spent money to portray yourself as someone you're not?" Once again, we return to the concept of getting real with ourselves.

And it's okay to ask questions, especially if you don't know. It's okay to say, "I need help."

So, let's take a look at what we need to know…and better still, what we need to do. Even though I can create budgets and recommendations for my clients and women just like you, I've also recognized that doing what I do is not powerful for you unless you apply it. What I mean by that is, will you take the committed action behind the knowledge you're learning in order to become powerful? My hope and mission is YES.

Maybe one simple commitment you can make is to print out your statements. Then take a look and see if any fees are being applied to you and make a phone call to reduce them or eliminate them altogether. Maybe it is to contact your cable provider because they accidentally charged you a little bit more instead of just letting it go.

One of my clients at my financial bootcamp told me, "By my printing out my statement and getting ready for this bootcamp, I realized HBO was charging me $50.00 a month more that I had not approved."

How powerful. I said, "We haven't even gotten started, and I already saved you 50 bucks a month."

So, you can see that knowledge is power when applied. One mistake I see women often make is to try to take care of everything all at once, instead of committing to something doable, like "Okay, today I'm just going to take care of that cable situation. Tomorrow I'm going to take care of my checking account statement."

Maybe you'll determine that you want to switch to a different cellular provider by deciding to compare rates and plans. I know I did. I was paying $130 a month with AT&T for years. So I went to T-Mobile, and now I pay $35.00 a month. So, I went from having a phone bill of $130 to now paying $35 a month. That saved me $95.00 a month that now goes directly into my savings.

You know what it took for me to make that decision? I had to let go of this conversation, "Well, I've been loyal to AT&T for 15 years." Who cares? Then, I had to drive to a T-Mobile provider and spend about an hour and a half making the switch. Think about that. If you take $95.00 and multiply that by 12 months. That's about $1,100. Multiply that by the 15 years that I've been doing this, and that's $17,000 I could have saved if I had just make that hour-and-a-half drive 15 years ago.

I've often thought about how much I'd like to have an account with that $17,000 in it. What about you? Are you willing to do what it takes to save money? You can find the time to fund your priorities. Do it on your lunch break and eat while you're there. Do it right after work. Do whatever it takes to make it happen. Recognize how important it is to take the time to implement the committed action to create the result you want (more money).

Create a plan with faith, confidence, commitment, knowledge, and *action*.

To succeed in anything, you must want it. You also need to have faith that you will see results, have confidence in your decisions, and show commitment to your plan. Most importantly, you must take action. If there is no action behind your words and beliefs, then nothing is going to get done.

When you're committed to your plan and save that pre-determined amount of money every single month, you're unstoppable. You're unstoppable because taking action and seeing your plan through is the most difficult and important part. Keep a positive attitude. Realize that you are in control of your money. That's when your money starts working very hard for you.

Start by paying yourself first.

With any financial goal, no matter how big or small, you must be sure to pay yourself first. Why? It's a matter of looking at your finances from different perspectives. If you were to get your paycheck and pay all of your utilities and credit cards before looking at the money you have left and paying yourself from that, you'll end up with less money overall. By shifting everything aside and saying, "I'm going to pay myself 10% first," you're building a consistent habit. This way, you control the amount of money that is going out to expenses such as your utilities and credit cards. You're building your financial freedom. It's important to note that by "pay yourself" I don't mean you should say, "I'm going to write myself a check, and I'm going to go spend it all at the mall." I mean put this money into a plan, a retirement plan, or a plan that you can easily access. Start saving now for the future.

Start following your financial plan as soon as possible. The younger you are, the better.

Your current age has a huge impact on your financial future. If you are younger, retirement is still a long way off and you have more time to prepare. For example, you could start by putting a lower amount away each month. It's also important to consider your spouse's age, particularly if he is much older or younger than you. His retirement age may be quite different from yours. Let's say you're 35 and you want to retire at 65. You have 30 years. But what if your spouse is 45? He actually only has 20 years. This will impact the amount of money that you can build up if you hadn't planned for retirement before.

The younger you start planning for the future, the more you can potentially have when you retire. You can also put smaller increments of money away because you still have time to build. However, if you have the extra money, go ahead and put in a larger amount. It never hurts to accumulate more quickly than you need to. Start building these habits at a young age. Realistically, your financial future will only work out if you are creating and choosing habits that support you and your lifestyle.

Commitment is the key element that makes financial planning work.

The most important element is commitment. Be committed to yourself. Be committed to knowing that you love yourself enough to save for the life you want…today and later in life. With commitment, dedication, and the other tools available to you, you can ultimately have an impact on your life as well as on your family's life. It's very important to remain committed and consistent. Commit to moving forward, and believe you can achieve your goals no matter what.

Use the convenience of automation so your plan works without worry.

Most importantly, pay yourself first! Pay your utility bills and your credit card bills at the end. Have a system in place, follow it consistently, and it will be running smoothly in no time. If you want less to worry about, create an automatic fund that serves your financial goal.

Think about it. When you wake up every morning, you're already on automatic. You get up, you brush your teeth, you go to the restroom, you have breakfast and coffee. That's automatic stuff. In order for your finances to run on automatic, you have to do the same thing over and over and over again. After a while, it will become second nature to you. You'll be thinking, "Oh yeah, that's all part of the process," and not, "Oh my God! I forgot to put money into my savings account again, and now I'm overdrawn." No! Don't settle for that. Be the person who says, "Everything's taken care of. This is just part of what I do." Make it part of your life.

With current technology, we now have apps on our phones that often make financial transactions quick and simple. Many banks allow you to pay your bills directly. Set everything on automatic so you never have to say, "Oh my god! I forgot to pay the gas bill," or "I forgot to pay my insurance bill." Don't put yourself through that. Use technology to your advantage. It's a tool that can support you and help create peace of mind. If your mortgage is due on the first, set it up so that the money is automatically debited out of your account before the deadline. This way, you don't have to think twice about it. Doing this also saves you money in every aspect. You're not paying late fees. You're also not paying additional postage to mail a check.

Make sure your system is easy to follow.

Finances do not need to be complex. As a matter of fact, if they're too complex for you to understand, they're probably not going to serve you or your family well. Money goes in, money goes out. Know when it's going out and what bucket it's going to. That's all. Don't make this more complicated than it needs to be. A lot of women will say, "This is a little too confusing for me." And I say, "Well, if you're feeling that way now, then something isn't working here." If you don't understand your own system, you can't make clear decisions regarding financial matters. If you have a financial coach, ask them to explain it in terms you'll understand. That's what they're there for. The bottom line is, do everything you can to make sure your system is easy to maintain and follow.

Believe you can achieve your goals.

Attitude is everything. It's very important to believe you can achieve your goals. If you can't see yourself being a part of this system, then it doesn't matter how well the system works. If you don't think you'll save enough to take vacations with your family and provide them financial freedom, then it doesn't matter how great the system is. Nothing is going to happen unless you believe in it. You have to say to yourself, "Yes, I can do this." We all have those friends who call us to go shopping more often than we want to or can afford to. It's okay for you to say no.

Surround yourself with family and friends who support your financial goals. When you feel like you're not on track, these are the people you can be open and honest with. You can go to them and say, "I'm falling off track. I want to establish financial freedom but I'm still shopping every day." They will support you and guide you back to the right path, no questions asked. Attitudes are contagious. Once you start telling yourself you can do it, you're also affecting the people around you and providing inspiration so they can believe they can do it, too.

Current choices will determine your future.

Let's just say that you've decided to forego all your financial goals. You're saying, "I don't have insurance, I don't have a retirement fund, I'm not a homeowner, and I don't have anything." All of those choices you make now will ultimately affect your future, whether it's in a positive or negative way. It's important to start making choices right now. If you don't choose now, time will pass, 10 years might pass, and pretty soon you'll be saying, "Oh my God, where did the time go?" In that time, you could have already had a retirement plan with $10,000 or $20,000, whatever you decided to put in there. You could have already given your family financial protection. Understand that you're making choices all the time, but your choices right now can have a huge impact on your future.

Use your paycheck (no matter the amount) to fund your future.

When using your paycheck to fund your future, you start by creating a plan. This will help familiarize you with the different options that are available. It doesn't matter how much money you're bringing in. As long as you start saving for your retirement, saving for your kids' college tuition, and saving to get out of debt, you have taken a huge step in the right direction. *Start* is the key word here. Once you do that, you've crossed the biggest hurdle for most people. No matter how much you're earning, stretch out that money as much as possible so you get the most out of it.

After you've taken that first step, everything seems a little easier. You'll think, "Oh yes, that's my plan. I know what I'm doing now." Having that plan allows you to start funding your future. You may not have a future without a plan. Choose to start saving and maintain those habits over time. Let's say you start a retirement account and decide to put in $5000 annually. You did it one year but didn't do it the following year, and then you decided to do it for three more years but skipped two years after that. That's not a good pattern to fall into. Being consistent with your money will allow you to fund your future and take your future in the direction you want it to go.

Life changes. So can your financial goals. Stay current with your experiences today.

Financial goals are fluid and malleable. Keep in mind that if your financial views have changed, you may need to change certain things in your financial future. However, that doesn't mean you have to change everything. If it's in your best interest to change it all, then do so. But like I've mentioned before, people don't always handle change very well. It's human nature. We don't like change. I hear that from clients all the time.

If your circumstances change, whether it's due to an engagement or a pregnancy or some other life-changing event, take the time to determine whether your prior financial plans still support your new future. If they do, keep them. If they don't, only change the portion that is necessary—the part that will allow you to support your new lifestyle. This change could be a recent marriage or a new baby in the family, but it could also be the death of a spouse or a newly empty nest.

Financial peace of mind means freedom from fear about money.

To have financial peace of mind, you need to look closely at how your money is being managed—in what areas is it working for you, and in what areas is it not? Look at how you are spending. Ask yourself if you're living the way you should be living, given your current income. If you make $5,000, are you spending $6,000? If you're making $5,000, are you living off $3,000?

Living beneath your means creates financial security. It all comes down to the choices you're making, the way your money is being spent, and how much you're spending. If your spending habits are working against you, you're probably not going to have peace of mind. On the other hand, if you see the results and know that they're working for you, you'll be able go to bed at night without so much uncertainty. You won't stay up worrying, "Oh my God, I forgot to pay the bills. Oh my God, I didn't pay this credit card. Oh my God, I don't make enough money," or whatever thoughts and fears usually consume your mind at the end of the night.

Take a good look at your finances. Don't just think, "I didn't pay this," or "I didn't do that." Those kinds of thoughts only make matters worse. Find a place to start, take action, and work from that point forward.

Embrace the struggle and move on.

Know where you are right now in terms of your financial future, and know that it's okay for you to be struggling. It's okay to feel like you've failed or feel like you aren't perfect or that your finances aren't in good shape. The most important part is knowing how you can get out of this funk.

Frequently, we will fight back or resist the current position we're in. But realistically, it's best to actually embrace our situation—to know what we did wrong and what still needs to be done. Being honest with ourselves allows us to move on.

I work with a lot of women who are constantly beating themselves up because everything didn't turn out the way it was supposed to. Guess what? It's okay. Failure is okay. In life, there isn't a manual that says, "Everything must be done exactly like *this*." Your finances are no different. Embrace your current situation. Say to yourself, "I am here. This is my current reality." By doing so, you can open and up and see what your needs are, and where you can improve.

Embrace the struggle, but don't wallow in it. Misery loves company. We often think, "This is what's going on with me, and I want everybody else around me to be in this space, too." But it's not about that. Financially, you got yourself in this situation. Don't feel sorry for yourself. Recognize that you need to figure out what bad choices you've made in the past, so that you can choose differently in the future. Everybody in your life will be happier for it.

Live and love in the now, but do so according to your financial plan.

While it's important to seize the day and to live in the now, you do have a responsibility, especially if you're a parent, to prepare for your family's future. You never know when your expiration date is going to come. If we all knew the exact date we were going to pass, then we would probably live life a bit differently. But the reality is that life is always surprising us.

So yes, you should try to live in the now with peace of mind, with love, with abundance, and with joy in your heart. Those are things that money can't buy. If your family is covered financially, regardless of what might happen to you, that knowledge can also bring you joy. Of course, they would miss you if you were gone, but you'd know that you did everything you could for their future.

This is where legacies are often left. You don't want to just die one day, with nobody to remember you. Just as you're living in the moment, just as you're loving them now, just as you're sharing that joy with them while alive, you can also pass your finances down to your family. Give them something to remember you by. Your loved ones will appreciate life a little bit more because they don't have the stress of thinking, "Oh my God, I have to go to work because I can't afford to take time off to mourn." Instead, they will feel blessed that you cared enough about them to leave this parting gift.

Remember the level of responsibility that we have as human beings. In order for you to really love other people, you need to be a selfless individual full of abundant love. Attaching a financial fund to express that love after your death is also a practical way to support your family.

Enjoy the process.

I've never understood why people are so reluctant to begin saving money for themselves. It's exciting to be able to say, "I'm taking financial responsibility for myself and my family!" You're saving money, and that can be a lot of fun. Once you start seeing your accounts grow, once you see your money being protected, and once you know how far you've come from having nothing is a great feeling. And now, you've created something that can ultimately give your family peace of mind.

So, take a moment to pat yourself on the back and enjoy the process. Nobody ever said that putting money away has to be such a serious and boring endeavor. Have fun with it! If you have a family, try to get your kids involved. Teach them how to recycle and how to earn their dollars. This way, they learn it from you. Sharing knowledge with others feels fantastic, especially if that knowledge was hard earned for you. Feel free to be creative, as long as it serves your purpose. Do whatever you need to if it'll save you the most amount of money.

And ladies, if you're not in the mood to deal with your finances, find a day when you *are* in the mood. Find a day when you're feeling your best and handle your finances then. It can be sad to see women handle their finances when they've had a very bad day. At the end of it, they're not paying attention, they've already checked out, or they're already thinking about what they're going to feed their families for dinner. Maybe they're only focusing on all these other conversations that are going on in their heads. It's very important to choose a day when you are feeling wonderful. Like the saying goes, "Put on your big girl panties," and get to work.

Create the future you want by putting money away now.

If right now, in your current financial situation, you are not able to put 100, 200, 300, 400 dollars away on a monthly basis, what makes you think that you'll be able to do it later when you're in your sixties? You may need even more then due to inflation because the cost of living is always going up. So, if you can't afford it now, you're not preparing yourself to receive anything in the future.

Some people set themselves and their families up so well that you start to hear about these trust fund babies. Their parents basically said, "We want to be able to provide for our family," and so they used the knowledge they had and put it into action. They believed they could do it, so they did.

You need to start believing that you can. You need to you start making sure that you're putting a little bit away now so you can create the future that you desire. By putting that money away now, it will ultimately pay off.

If you get off track, just get yourself back on.

Too often, families will be saving their money routinely until they are suddenly blindsided by serious financial issues. If this has ever happened to you, you know this is why it's so important to have different buckets or different little nest eggs for everything. In case of emergency, make sure to have an emergency fund that is immediately accessible. If you're unable to save for a few months because of a large emergency expense, try to get back on track as soon as possible. The longer you wait, the more you'll have to put away later on. Usually, you end up with less in the long run because if you stop saving consistently, your money isn't going to build up solidly. Even if you don't feel the consequences immediately, you will definitely pay the price later. Trust yourself and say, "Look, I didn't save for four months. It's time for me to get back on track."

Chapter Three

BUDGETS AND BUCKETS
AND OPTIONS...OH MY

To a certain extent, it doesn't matter how much
money you make. What really matters is
how you're spreading that money.

Now that you know the answers to your important financial questions, the value of saving money, how much your expenses are, the need to commit to a financial plan, and all the rewards that come with doing so, it's time to create your budget. And that's exactly what happens during my second visits with my clients for exactly the same reasons. We first needed to find out where they were, so they could plan what to do next.

One of the best things about having a monthly budget that provides for your financial security is that it can also provide for what you want today. When you are aware of what you are bringing in, then you can budget in a way that minimizes the feeling of "sacrifice." I want you to get your nails done if it makes you happy. I want you to buy that new outfit because you want to look great at a party or on a date...or just because. I want you to have the car or the house that you love. I want you to be able to fund your priorities. Following a monthly budget means you're allotting enough money to support and enjoy all the areas of your life right now. The goal is to be able to have it all.

So, let's get started.

Your money. Your budget. Your life.

I have created an easy-to-use financial planning and budget system that divides your net income into percentages for each category that funds your life. I like to call them "buckets." You designate a certain percentage to each bucket. Then, within each bucket, there are different categories, and within each category, there are different options. It sounds like a lot, I know, but remember...*the goal is to be able to have it all.*

Bucket One: Housing (35% of Net Income)
- Rent/Mortgage
- HOA Fees
- Homeowners or Renters Insurance

Bucket Two: Living Expenses (20%)
- Food
- Entertainment
- Utilities
- Gasoline
- Cellular Service
- Cable or Another TV Provider
- Internet
- School Supplies

- Beauty and Personal Care
- Day Care or School Fees

Bucket Three: Transportation (15% of Net Income)
- Automobile Payments
- Automobile Insurance
- Public Transportation
- Taxi, Uber, or Lyft Fees

Bucket Four: Debt (15% of Net Income)
- Student Loans
- Credit Card Loans
- Personal Loans

Bucket Five: Savings (15% of Net Income)
- Emergency Fund
- Retirement
- Children's College Fund
- Life Insurance

Now let's look at each bucket, each category, and the options available to you under each one. For the purposes of this example, let's assume a net monthly income of $5,000.

Bucket One: Housing (35% of Net Income)

Ask yourself what you can afford. That's really what it comes down to. Take a look at your paycheck. This is the choice you made when you chose your job and chose to earn a certain income. Now choose the rent or mortgage payment that can support that amount. If you want a bigger house, then find a way to make more money or adjust your financial budget so more can go toward housing. During the 2008 financial meltdown, a lot of people lost their homes because they could no longer afford them. That doesn't support a family, and it doesn't support the economy. Make sure you know where you stand in terms of your mortgage, so you can always afford to pay it.

With a net monthly of income of $5,000, this means you'd have $1,750 to spend on housing each month. And you have two options: Owning or Renting. So, whether you are considering buying a home or renting, keep in mind that what you can afford is $1,750 each month. And that includes any additional housing expenses, such as HOA fees, renter's insurance, or homeowner's insurance.

If you do want to be a homeowner, having the ability to save money to buy a home is a blessing. My recommendation is to save the usual 20% for a down payment, but there are some first-time homebuyer programs that allow you to fund with less than that, usually around 3.5% or 5%. If that means putting $300 or $500 or whatever you can afford to save toward your down payment each month, then that's where you start. You might want to sell or buy something that supports those financial needs. Before you know it, you'll have your down payment on your own home.

Bucket Two: Living Expenses (20% of Net Income)

In the list of living expenses, which varies according to any individual's needs, the two biggest areas of expense are food and entertainment, so let's take a look at those in greater detail.

Food

I love to eat out, but I also enjoy meal prepping (when it's simplified). I'm a newlywed, so I create an experience of it in order to have fun. I'll say to my husband, "Let's cook together."

The one thing I don't love is going to the supermarket to buy food. I felt it was a waste of my time, I didn't know which foods to choose in order to make a meal, and often I'd get home and be missing one or several of the ingredients for the recipe. I'm no chef by any means. Something I recently joined was a food delivery service. You select certain meals and the ingredients are delivered to you in the right proportions, so you don't have to waste any food. You use all of their products, and it's three meals per week. And they're organic, healthy, and delicious, and it fuels my soul. It fuels everything about who you are, and it's fun to prepare these meals with my husband and discover new recipes.

This was a great discovery for me, and it may work for you, too. The delivery service is about $100 a week for three healthy meals, rather than spending possibly $100 or more for one meal together at a restaurant that may not support my lifestyle. Or I could go to the market and buy $100 of food that may not include the right ingredients to make anything well.

Another drawback of grocery shopping can be impulse buying. For me, I could easily end up buying cereal and a gallon of milk because it's convenient or buying something I don't need because it looks good. The milk would end up spoiling, and I'd end up feeling guilty about food I ended up throwing away. Remember, throwing away food is just like throwing away money. There was also the sense of guilt around imagining the people who could've eaten that food.

So again, know your different options and plan your food expenses accordingly. If eating out is your choice, then eat out and don't buy the food that's just going to sit and waste in your refrigerator. And always remember your food expense budget and stick to it.

Entertainment

Many of my clients think they have to spend so much money to entertain themselves, but that's just not true. There are many free events going on in different communities all the time. I live in the city of Whittier. I have my business in the city of Whittier. But I can tell you, I have been to free concerts at the park in other cities. I have gone to Jazz festivals in different cities. I've attended different events hosted by cities throughout my local area.

I happen to host free vision board workshops, but I know a lot of different locations that host many free workshops of a wide variety. I know some gyms that will give you a one-week pass for free...what a great way to use a gym for free before choosing to join.

There are so many different things out there. It's just a matter of going online or the local city page and seeing what's out there. We often don't take the time to do that because we think we always must pay for entertainment, right? But people and groups and associations create all kinds of free entertainment for you. And so, as you've been seeing me say throughout this book, pay attention. Take a minute to just say, "Let's see what I can create. Let's see what's out there that'll cost me nothing."

Once again, this is another example of having a monthly budget with different categories and options, so you can be flexible. One month you may want to attend a concert or the ballet or a comedy club. Budget for it. If you spend nothing on entertainment one month, those savings can go to purchase a big-ticket event the month.

Bucket Three: Transportation (15% of Net Income)

Who doesn't like driving a nice car? I constantly hear people say, "Oh, I don't care if I can afford it; it looks so great." That's not the point. The point is you need a plan that will support your method of transportation.

Normally, you should be applying about 15% of your income toward transportation. This includes car payments, gas, insurance, and repairs. If your net monthly income is $5,000, and you decide, "Well, I look great in this beautiful car, and I'm going to spend $1,400 a month to keep it," then that will not work for you. That's not a sustainable plan. Over time, that vehicle is going to become so stressful to maintain that it won't be worth it. So, live within your means and make sure that only 15% of your income is applied toward transportation. With a $5,000 net income, that means $750 total.

There are also three options to consider in the transportation category: buy a new car, buy a used car, or lease a car. Which one's better for you?

My parents said, "Don't ever lease a car. That is just so bad. It's like paying for someone else's car." And they were right. Leasing may make sense in the short term…meaning, a smaller monthly payment. However, in the long run, you may be losing out. Instead, buy a used car to keep your payments affordable, and at the end of paying off the loan you'll have a car that you own.

But, then there's the ego part of you that can kick in, "I want a new car. I love the new car smell." Because of course you deserve a new car, absolutely. But when it depreciates 30% as soon as your drive that puppy out, it's like, "Ew, okay, maybe I don't really need a new car. Maybe I should just get that used car that doesn't have a whole lot of miles." That's what I did. I bought a used car from a dealer, which I had never done before. But when I bought it and drove it off the lot, I thought, "I just saved myself $50,000. This totally makes sense." Why? Because it made sense for what I'm creating for myself.

But if you were to ask me this about 10 years ago, I'd have been right there with you about buying that new car. My conversations weren't about self-love and funding my priorities, they were more like, "But I want it, and won't I look good driving that car?" I truly believe that we go through different conversations depending on our different ages in our lives. I'm going to be 37 next week, and I'm much happier and more financially free with my reasonable car payments than I was driving around in a glitzy new car.

Bucket Four: Debt (15% of Net Income)

Debt often causes people a lot of stress. When I ask, "Well, do you have a system in place to pay it off?" clients often respond with, "Well, no, I just pay more than my minimum payment." Unfortunately, paying more than your minimum payment doesn't guarantee you'll get out of debt any more quickly. This is a very common misconception. I see it all the time. People will say, "Well, my minimum payment is only $100, but I send in $300." Great! But that's not enough. You need a plan. You need a system.

Once again, assuming a $5,000 monthly net income, you should be paying at least $750 toward any debt and even more if you can afford it. Let's say your minimum payments total $250, you could easily send more if you follow your budget. Don't fall into the trap of thinking that's taking money away from yourself, because you're actually funding it into this bucket to create financial freedom for yourself even sooner.

In order to pay off your debt, create a long-term plan to follow. Let's say you have five credit cards. The one with the lowest balance is $500, and the other ones are at $1000, $2000, $4000, and $6000. You should try to pay off the smaller amounts first. These mini victories will give you the confidence to say, "Oh, I did it once. I can do it again." Or, "Yes, I didn't think I would ever get there. Now I know I can."

When you think you can, you will. Suddenly, even the larger amounts don't look so terrifying anymore.

Even though 15% of your income should be applied toward debt, it doesn't mean you have to *be* in debt. Just because the word *debt* exists doesn't mean that you have to have it! Imagine if you owed nothing so you could apply that 15% toward something else.

Set a date for yourself and say, "By this date, I will be financially free." If you don't set that specific goal, the debt will drag on. A lot of people don't even know what it's like to live debt-free because, for them, being in debt is the norm. Figure out how long it's going to take you to pay off the debt and stick to the schedule you've set.

Remember, when I say debt, I'm talking about student loans, credit card loans, and personal loans. How much money do you owe? I'm talking about all of it. If you have student loans, find a way to pay them off. Credit card debt? Find a way to pay it off. Personal loans? Pay back your friends and family. Once that happens, don't use the percentage of income you were setting aside for debt to apply to new debt. Shift that money instead—put it towards something you can use. You might want to get a slightly bigger house or save for a family vacation or put the extra money into your savings accounts. It's possible to live without debt! A strong financial plan can ultimately give you peace of mind.

Keep in mind though, there is a difference between "good debt" and "bad debt." Good debt is housing. For example, when you get a mortgage payment, you know that when you eventually pay it off, you'll have equity. It can support you in various ways. A student loan is another example of "good debt" as it is an investment in your career. But with a credit card, you can spend, spend, and spend some more. You're giving money to a credit card company for buying things that usually don't really support you.

Ladies, you probably know what I'm talking about. You want to buy a new pair of expensive shoes, so you say, "Oh, I'll just put it on credit." Over time, you slowly realize you've bought 10 pairs of shoes you don't really need or even wear anymore. That's bad debt. Why? Because it doesn't add value to your financial plan. A mortgage, on the other hand, brings value because it builds equity. Buying shoes or other things you don't need only gives you instant gratification.

So, remember, good debt builds equity and gives you something at the end of the day. Bad debt doesn't give you anything...except maybe headaches and a lot of stress.

Bucket Five: Savings (15% of Net Income)

Even though this bucket represents only 15% of your income, it is the most important bucket because in order to achieve financial freedom, *you must pay yourself first.* If you don't, you're going to end up broke and living off of Social Security (if it still exists), just like my parents. That's just the harsh reality. When you finally retire, you won't have enough money to live. Don't let this happen to you.

Pay yourself a minimum of 10%, but I recommend 15%. And if you can afford it, pay yourself 20%. You'll never regret putting more money away. And when I say pay yourself first, I don't mean to go shopping and then pay your bills. I mean that you should make sure you have an account that you can't access now—one that's going to be available for you when you get older and retire, no matter what that age is. Paying yourself first means don't touch that 15% or 20%.

When you pay yourself first, it's wonderful to know you have options for savings based on what's important to *you*. Let's look at the different categories and options for saving well. Again, we'll use 15% of $5,000 which is $750. That $750 must be divided into three different categories (four if you have children and want to help fund their education).

Category One: Emergency Account

What I mean by an emergency account is money that can be used for a true emergency that you have immediate access to. Not a credit card. Not a CD. Not your retirement account. Not your kid's college education fund. It is literally money in a savings account that you can pull out *in case of emergency.* Nobody ever told me to have an emergency account. I was like, "An emergency account, what do you mean?"

Well, I now know what it means. You create an emergency fund "just in case." There are some very lucky people who've never experienced a downfall, or a layoff from a job, or a serious illness, or a blown engine gasket. And since they've never experienced losses, they just continue to spend and maybe cross their fingers. But this book is about financial awareness and paying attention, so please pay big attention to this!

I recommend that you always have between six months' to a year's worth of emergency money set aside. If that sounds like too much to you, then start by putting three months away. I've known many clients and friends who get bogged down with despair. They'll say, "Oh my God, I need to put away a year's worth of money? I won't be able to do that!" So, they give up before they even get started. But I know if you're reading this book, you're not one of those people, right?

If you feel overwhelmed, take baby steps. If you don't have any emergency funds right now, start slowly. Tell yourself, "Well, I'm going to start by saving up one month." Once you've done that, you've given yourself a confidence boost. After that, you're going to want to do it again with pride. And then you save another month. In no time at all, you may have saved up to three months. Start slowly, stay consistent, and watch your savings grow to your goal of six months to a year.

Another way to build up your emergency funds is by saving any extra money that comes in. If you inherit money or get a tax refund, put those away instead of spending them. Build those up. Your emergency account can definitely save you from stressful situations and even financial ruin. The knowledge that money is there "just in case" will allow you to breathe easier. Start saving. Take it one step at a time. That's the best advice I can give you.

There is one other option you can consider, but only if you're good at not using credit cards. As I've mentioned, you want the ability to access any emergency funds right away. I am not saying that a credit card is the best emergency account, but if you have a credit card with no balance, that can be an option. If you do use a credit card, make sure that you have money available when the credit card balance is due so you can add those payments into your monthly debt expenses.

Category Two: Retirement Account

With retirement savings, it is important to know that this is a savings account that goes to your retirement on top of Social Security benefits. On top of 401ks. On top of pension plans. Why? Because when you do retire, you will have multiple streams of income coming in from different sources. And then you can live your retirement the way you want on the money you worked hard to save.

To provide a solid plan, you need to invest in a system of different accounts: pre-tax, post-tax, and cash-value life insurance (which is also post-tax). In everything, you have diversification, but it's essential to own an insurance account, especially if you have kids. You will protect your life, protect your home, and protect your kids' future college goals if the same percentage of your income that goes to the first two accounts is also going into the insurance bucket. Based on our assumption of 15% of $5,000 net monthly income, that means you would be putting $250 in pre-tax, $250 in post-tax, and $250 in cash-value life insurance.

Some employers will provide them, and some won't. Even if your employer provides you with a 401k, 403b, or 457, remember that you also have the option of choosing another account outside of work, whether it's a traditional or Roth IRA. And even if your employer provides term life insurance, you can still do a cash-value insurance policy and ultimately supplement a portion of your retirement.

For some people, it's best to go pre-tax because that will minimize the amount of taxes that they need to pay right now. For others, it makes much more sense to go ahead and pay all their taxes now, so they can let the income that they're saving grow over a period of time.

Know what your tax bracket is. The vast majority of tax brackets are now at 25% to 28%. By knowing what your current tax situation is, you may decide to go post-tax because you're at your lowest tax bracket now. People often say, "But it's better to get a pre-tax account." Based on what information? Most people are married, have a house, have kids—those are the three largest write-offs that you'll ever have in your life. All three can reduce your tax bracket. But if you're single, you might decide that going pre-tax will allow you to pay less on taxes.

Everything should be based on your unique situation. Make sure you have a very good relationship with your CPA or your tax preparer, so that you can ask questions and get involved.

Honestly, post-tax is one of my favorites. I like it when people pay their taxes now, especially if they're married, are homeowners, or have children. Pay your taxes now. Take advantage of those write-offs now because nobody knows what taxes are going to look like in 10, 20, 30, or 40 years.

I know my parents weren't expecting to pay a 25% tax bracket. But even though I personally prefer post-tax, if the situation warrants it, I will sometimes tell people, "It's important for you to put money away pre-tax because this supports you in getting the financial results you want." Know that your money ultimately gets diversified into different options that will support your financial goals. As with any part of financial planning, it all depends on what your goals are.

In addition to weighing the benefits of post- or pre-tax options for retirement, clients often don't realize that using a cash-value license insurance plan can support your goals as well. There are many cash-value life insurance policies. Find the one that gives you more for your buck. Understand how these cash-value life insurances work. Some of them may give you low rates of about 3% to 4%. Others may have higher fixed amounts.

Cash-value life insurance can also protect your family up until the age of 120. This means you're basically getting life insurance for life. The cash-value component also allows you to build an income by overfunding these insurance policies, all while protecting your family. A portion of the money you're overfunding will be going into one bucket. That bucket is what's protecting your family, making sure that you have insurance until the age of 120.

The other bucket that's growing is the cash-value side of it. As this cash-value side grows, depending on when you started and how many years you've been with the plan, you have money available in an account that you can easily access. These accounts are normally post-taxed, so you've already paid taxes on that money. That's why you're able to access this fund. These accounts don't work like a bank account with an ATM, but it's a similar concept. At any point, you can dip into the bucket and say, "Okay, I've had this policy for 20 years. How much cash value have I accumulated in that time?"

At the same time, you're able to use that cash value to take a vacation, to find a place of your own, to help start up a business—whatever your goals may be. But if something were to happen to you, you'd know that your family was protected at all times because this policy covered you from the time you passed and/or up until you would've been 120.

Make sure you know how each retirement account is going to support your family and supplement retirement. Do your homework on these companies and their available accounts. Take the time to ensure that any additional plans you choose will also work with the existing plan you have with your employer.

Category Three: Life Insurance

People often want to know how they can enjoy their money now and still protect their family when they die. I love getting this question because it tells me that they are thinking of the future and truly want to protect their family to the best of their ability. At the same time, they still want to enjoy life as it comes. Striking a balance is important.

I used to think of life insurance as that stereotypical car salesman who was just trying to take my money. Honestly, that was my interpretation of life insurance, and that's why I never wanted to talk to people about life insurance. It was one of those things you just didn't talk about, just like money. At least culturally, for me, those are conversations you never had during family dinners or any other time for that matter. Never, ever do I remember having financial conversations with my family—not with my parents, my brothers, or my sisters, and I'm the youngest of eight.

Yet, I have seen multiple times that death shatters lives. Different dreams are just destroyed. I have a friend who was studying to become a doctor. And then his father died of a heart attack. He was the oldest son, so guess what? He needed to stop his dreams and everything he planned in order to provide for his Mom. Because his Mom was not in mental capacity to do that. So, his life stopped because his father died. I doubt his father meant for that to happen.

But, based on the number of clients that I have seen, it's a common story. I don't think we understand how to use life insurance as leverage to make sure that we and our loved ones are taken care of and protected.

For example, there are life insurance policies that have terminal illness riders in them. If you were to become terminally ill and have less than two years to live, the policy pays you a portion of the death benefit, usually the lowest of either 10% or $100,000, while you're still living. That way, you can pay medical bills without worry or spend some money on some of your final wishes, like the dream vacation you always meant to take but never could.

With that type of life insurance policy, you're able to do that. But if you don't have that, then where do you get money from in your final days?

I have a client who is in her mid-thirties and was diagnosed with terminal cancer. She wanted to get life insurance after she had been diagnosed, but unfortunately and tragically, she can't do that. If she had done so before she had cancer, and because of the amount of time that they have given her, she would have been able to take out a portion of the death benefit and maybe fulfill some dream or travel to somewhere luxurious. Or maybe she could have spent the money on additional experimental treatments that might have helped her. She could have at least had the financial resources to be able to support herself during her illness. I pray that you are never in a position to think, "I wish I had gotten that insurance." I've seen it happen too many times that people don't understand the leverage of life insurance until they're placed in the position to need it.

It is imperative that you understand how life insurance, if used and leveraged properly, can enormously benefit you while you're alive and obviously upon passing.

For those who are wealthy, usually it's because genera-tions through generations understood the value of being properly protected. They made sure that out of nothing they created something, and even more was created from that. They don't just focus on their business and that's it. No, they focus on their family's well-being because, the smart business owner knows, their family's well-being is equally as important as the well-being of their business.

At this point, you might be wondering, "What are my options for life insurance?" The reality is that everybody's situation is different. It's not that some plans are definitively better than others. Ultimately, you should choose the plan that will best support your family and your financial needs. As always, you must do your homework. Many types of insurances exist. Know which policies you can afford as well as which policies can protect your family if something happens to you.

Let's take a look at some of the most common plans.

Term Life

Term life insurance is normally the least expensive kind of insurance. I've been able to find plans that, if something happens to their family, they've locked in their rate for 30 years. The longer term you get, the longer you ensure that your monthly premium is not going to increase.

Cash-Value Insurance

As I mentioned in the retirement category, there is also cash-value life insurance that you have to overfund, so you're putting more money into it. But some people cannot afford these policies due to that need to overfund them. I have spoken to families who cannot afford these cash-value life insurance policies, but it's wise to shop around. There are many insurance companies that offer different policies. Some may charge a higher premium and have a higher health ratings cost. Do your homework. Meet with a professional to see what your available options are. If there's a financial benefit, whether your family gets more protection or maybe just pays less, that's important knowledge to have.

Disability and Long-Term Care Insurance

These are insurances where people often say, "Well, I don't know if I have it. I'm not sure if my employer provides me with this." Or maybe those two insurances are optional plans you can purchase through your employer at a group rate. Or you can purchase them on your own.

It's important to examine these insurance options because people are living longer now than they used to. These types of insurance exist to protect us in case we need assistance from others in our old age. Particularly if you're single and have no children—who's going take care of you when you're older? In many situations people will say, "My long-term care didn't support my needs." Fine. But know that you have it, just in case of emergency. That's the whole purpose of insurance. It will be there for you when you need it. So, make sure you consider all your options.

Homeowner's Insurance

As with any type of insurance, it's important for you to shop around and know your options. Know how much you're paying on insurance. Take a look at your homeowner's insurance annually. Know your specific needs. That way, if you need a little more coverage or if you need a little bit less, you can make changes accordingly.

General Insurance Advice

Do a thorough analysis of all your insurance plans. You go to the doctor annually to get a physical exam, and it's very important you practice the same care with your insurance plans. Read them, page by page, and make changes if it benefits you and your family.

A lot of people fear change. But if a new plan saves you money and making the change is suitable, then do it. Nothing is set in stone. You don't have to stay with the same insurance forever just because you purchased it once. If you're happy with what you've got, that's great. But if it makes more sense for you to switch over, then that's what you need to do. Be sure you know why you're switching. Don't randomly do it just because someone tells you to. Know what the financial benefit will be for you personally.

Insurance and Taxes

When people inherit life insurance money, it's tax-free. That's the beautiful part. If someone passes away and leaves you $250,000, that money is tax-free for you because the insurance was paid for with post-tax money. In other words, they used money from their checking account, which was money they already paid taxes on. It's wonderful to know that when you do get a life insurance plan, your beneficiaries are going to be receiving it tax-free.

CASE STUDY: Leveraging Life Insurance

A husband and wife came into my office. They have $85,000. They both said this money is for their children. They wanted to leave a legacy for them, so they wanted to divide the $83,000 into three so each child gets an equal share.

That sounds really nice.

So, $83,000 divided by three people. They thought, "We're going to leave our kids with $27,600 each." That's what they thought. But they had no idea that this money was within a pension plan, and they would not be able to just transfer the pension fund directly to each child without their children having to pay taxes on it.

So, if you multiply $83,000 times 20% in taxes (as an average) that means that realistically their $83,000 just became $66,000. Which means that each child is going to get about $22,000. Of course, $22,000 is better than nothing. But the interesting thing they said was, "Well 100% of this money is for legacy building. That's what we call it, legacy building." "Yes," I said, "but, why don't we do this? Why don't we take your $83,000, put it into a lifetime annuity that will pay you a check for the rest of your life up until you pass away?"

The amount of the paycheck they'd receive was $350 a month. They said, "That sounds great. But, that doesn't leave the money to our kids. I don't want to divide $350 in three different ways every single month."

Our conversation continued. I said, "Okay hear me out. If you put the $83,000 into a lifetime annuity, what will happen is we're going to get you a life insurance policy that is going to be for $150,000 instead."

Now the only way this plan would make sense is if the medical results to obtain the life insurance come back favorable to him. It just so happened that the results did. The husband was in the best of health. This gentleman is 62, and because of that his life insurance was going to cost $355 a month.

"What do you mean?" he asked. I said, "You're going to have to pay $5.00 out of pocket but hear me out. Now when you die and transfer your legacy, instead of only transferring $22,000 to each child, you now have converted it because of the leverage of life insurance. Now each one of your children will receive $50,000 on top of any money left over in the annuity."

"Wow, is that possible?" they asked. "Of course it is, absolutely it's possible."

So, I told them that if they're going to transfer a legacy to their children the way they want to, you may be limiting them instead of taking a moment and an opportunity to say, "What do I get to do to be able to leave my legacy and transfer this wealth in a way that my children can ultimately have more?" I get it, the children are like, "We want you to enjoy your money. We don't want this money, obviously coming from you guys, this is for you." However, the parents were not going to use it. They didn't need it. They had a surplus already. So, I created $50,000 per child out of $83,000.

That is how you can use life insurance as legacy. For their children, maybe they won't need it when their father passes, but what if their kids need it? What if that $50,000 could be used to fund their grandkids to go to school or to open a business? Or maybe they could donate it to a charity of choice.

That's how you strategically use life insurance as leverage.

Category Four: Children's College Savings

Saving for your children's education is a major goal for many parents. And one of the best features of a child's college fund is that you can begin when they're two weeks old. And as with all the accounts I've discussed, earlier is always better.

Remember too that saving for your child is a portion of that 15% you're going to save each month to fund all your priorities. So, when deciding how much to save, it's very important to know when you're going to start and how much you want to support your kids with their education. I know parents who want to put $1,200 away in college tuition on a monthly basis, and so they just do it. And then there are other families who put $20 away over time, knowing that they're starting early. The money will eventually build up.

Age is another consideration when deciding how much money you should apply toward a child's college savings plan...yours as well as theirs. If you start when your kid is only two weeks old then, of course, you can start with a lower amount. But if your kids are already ten years old, then you're going to need to put more money away.

Ask yourself where you see your son or daughter going to college. Ask yourself how much you're willing to support your child to make it happen. College tuition is constantly getting more expensive. Inflation will also kick in the years ahead. After considering these factors, then you can start working backwards to determine how much you want to put away.

For parents who do want to save for their children's college tuition, many options are available to you. There are 529 plans that a lot of families use for college plans. There are also additional things, such as the cash-value life insurances we've discussed. Often, the cash value can be used as supplemental funding for college tuition. There are a few additional options available, but 529s and cash-value insurances are two of the best.

More often than not, we hope our kids will to go to college. But what if they decide to start their own business after high school? Or what if they just decide, "Mom, I don't want to go to college"? Because that does happen. They might want to join the Marines instead. Regardless of your child's choice after high school, you should always be prepared.

Teaching your kids about savings and leading by example is a blessing. Doing so will also teach your son or daughter to take on that responsibility with their own kids. But make sure your children are aware that it's also their responsibility to save for a portion of their college tuition. They should know the need to apply for grants and scholarships and not rely on mom and dad to pay for everything. When your child is able to say, "I'm going to apply, and I can do this," it's a huge confidence booster. Your child could also develop the discipline to take action because they think, "I'm going to be the best at this, so this how I'll get the money to pursue it."

At the end of the day, if you're unable to come up with the money in time, don't feel bad. If your friends are putting away more than you, don't feel bad about that either. But do take the time to communicate with your children and let them know that—financially speaking—you don't want them to end up like you with the same financial mistakes. You want them to be better. You want them to be informed so they can do those things that you, as a parent, didn't get a chance to do.

Understand that wanting to help your kid is a wonderful thing. They'll be grateful for any amount that you're able to give them.

Some Final Thoughts on a Critical Expense

Frequently in the Latin culture, family members will stop talking to each other—all because of disagreements regarding money. Maybe it's not strictly a Latin thing, but I know I've seen it happen within my own family. People die. What follows are endless arguments about how things should have been. You know... "Grandma wanted this." "No, Grandma wanted that." Why go through all of that when you can save time by creating a will and a trust?

We all know death is coming eventually. I call it our expiration date. When that happens, you know that nobody will ever be able to replace you. That's why it's vital to make sure that your final wishes are noted in a safe place, such as a will or trust.

Let's say that you have three kids. You want all three of your kids to get equal portions of your home after you pass. They can choose to sell it and then equally distribute the funds. Or, you could write in your will that, "I want them to sell the property, and I want all the proceeds to go to a nonprofit organization." Whatever your wishes are, they can be granted as long as you leave them in writing.

Yes, the cost of these documents can often be expensive. Hiring an attorney to support you in setting up a trust can ultimately save your family from the chaos and disagreements. Additionally, you'll have peace of mind knowing that all your wishes will be granted even after you're no longer here. If you want to protect your assets and your family, don't delay in getting this done.

Chapter Four

REDUCE CURRENT PAYMENTS AND SAVE MORE MONEY...EVERY SINGLE MONTH

If you find a different provider that better supports your financial goals, make the switch. It's not about the companies. It's about you, your family, and your finances.

Too often, we run our lives and finances on automatic. If that applies to regularly paying ourselves by saving 15% of our income each month, that's a great thing. But sometimes, because of not paying attention, parts of our finances fall to automatic settings that we don't even bother to check. I had a client recently confess that the automatic deductions from her checking account (for things like a membership site that she never engages in and subscriptions to things she long ago stopped reading) were things she kept *planning* to use so she kept the deductions as some sort of incentive to do so. But it never worked.

So, guess what I did? I pointed out the money she was paying for nothing and asked her what else she could do with that money instead? She canceled them right then and there during her first visit to my office. She saved herself about $450 a year from that simple action.

There are many things we can do to save a little more money as well as make a little more money. And who doesn't want more money? Let's check out some easy ways to do just that.

Reduce your utilities, phone, and cable bills.

You have many ways to drastically save money on these monthly living expenses. First, when you receive a new bill, be sure to examine it carefully because you might find extra charges on there. Sometimes it pays to call the company and ask what those extra charges are for. If it's an error, they will credit that charge. Same thing with your cable and phone bills.

Maybe the price of these services increased, but you didn't notice because you weren't checking your bills. You can ask if they offer special programs to help families save money. Also, sometimes just calling to get a reduced cost works, too! Do your research. Look into those plans! If you're spending a lot on your phone bills, consider changing your provider and getting a cheaper plan, particularly if you have kids who are included in the family plan. Ask yourself, "Where can I pay the least amount of money?" Set limits on your kids' cell phone usage as well. Have a frank discussion with them and lay down the ground rules: "You'll be able to use X number of minutes each month on this plan because that's what we can afford."

Don't just stick with your original providers because you don't want the hassle of calling or switching. If you find a different provider that better supports your financial goals, make the switch. I did that with my own cell service. I had been a "loyal" customer for years to my cell provider, and my reward was that I paid more and more, year after year. When I took the time to research and switch, I saved myself $95 a month. That's $1,140 year I earned from an hour of my time.

Have fun for less.

As we talked about in Chapter 3, there are many ways to entertain your family without overspending. Spend time at the park on a nice day. Find out when the local museum or zoo is offering a free day. Check local listings for free outdoor concerts. Take a look at the flyers on your community bulletin boards and keep an eye out for newsletters that advertise free events. Take advantage of all these free opportunities that have been created. You'll also have the extra benefit of getting to know your neighbors and your city.

You don't necessarily need to go out to entertain your family. You could stay home and play board games or create your own unique family time. You don't have to overspend to do that. Ask yourself what will make your family happy. If you're willing to pay for your entertainment, just make sure to set a strict budget for it. If you love to go to the movies, take advantage of matinee prices. Remain aware of how much you're spending each month, but still have plenty of fun.

Don't pay more than you have to for a vehicle.

There are ways to save time and money when purchasing a vehicle regardless if it's new or pre-owned. But it also takes time and money to drive around to different car dealerships. So, before you set out to the dealers, do your research online about the type of car you want and the price ranges. Then write out a letter explaining what you're looking for, what your price range is, and other specifics like that. Take it to the car dealers and say, "This is what I'm looking for. If you have something that fits the bill, I'm willing to spend the time and the money it takes to make a purchase because I'm a serious buyer."

Use this same letter at about five different dealers. The dealer who calls you back and is willing to work with the numbers that you set—this is the dealer you go to. Do your homework ahead of time! Car-buying can often be such a headache, and people will spend all day doing it. They end up at the dealership forever. Or they're pressured into buying something that doesn't fit their original specifications.

Do yourself a favor and make certain decisions prior to your visit. That way, you'll walk in and the dealers will already be expecting you. They'll be familiar with the numbers you talked about over the phone in the comfort of your own home. You're going in to take a look at your car, sign your contract, and then drive away. Make the trip as quick and smooth and *inexpensive* as possible.

Compromise with yourself on daily pleasures like Starbucks.

Sometimes people want to save money, but they aren't willing to give up the little things in life that bring them comfort—like their daily cup of coffee at their favorite coffee house. Well, you could start making coffee at home for part of the week. Consider having coffee at home every day except Friday. Maybe on Fridays, you allow yourself to go out and splurge a little. That's called a compromise.

Use discounts and coupons…regardless if you can "afford" to pay full price.

You don't have to pay full price for anything just because you can afford it. Everyone loves a good sale. Everyone loves a discount. And yet, there are some people who think they're being "cheap" by taking advantage of cost-cutting opportunities. Don't feel cheap. It doesn't hurt anyone to save whenever and wherever you can.

Let's say you decide to buy a pair of shoes that are priced at 50% off. But if you're able to afford the difference, then put that extra money away into a savings fund. That's not being cheap. That's being wise with your money. Invest what you saved and make your money start working for you.

Get over emotional attachments.

As you know by now, many families don't take the time to sit down and actually look at their current budget. As a result, they don't really know what their money can do for them. Clients sometimes tell me, "Well, I don't make a lot of money, but I want to get out of debt." To that I say, "Great! Let's take a look at what you're doing with your money right now."

We then find out that they're spending less toward minimum payments and credit cards while spending a lot more on entertainment or the gym or going out to expensive restaurants. Next, I say, "What if we shifted the money you were putting into this particular credit card or the money that you were using for the gym and put it toward one of your other credit card debts that has a higher interest rate? That way you'll get out of this debt first, but by using that same money."

It's crazy but true…normally, people don't do this because they're emotionally attached to their money and can't see the light at the end of the tunnel. So, I tell them, "I'm here to give you a neutral perspective about this. I'm not emotionally attached to your money. Most of the time, I actually know where your money is going just because I can see it. I can figure out where your values are depending on where your money is being spent." Use your current budget to help you live your true values. For some people, the goal is getting out of debt; for others, it's saving more money. Remember, ultimately you can have it all.

Take steps to reduce your interest rates.

Be sure to have a plan and know your interest rates. Most people know how much they spend on a monthly basis, but they don't know anything else. They don't know how much interest they're paying. Once they sit down with me and realize they owe $5,000 and their interest rate is at 27.99%, that's a huge eye-opener. I've even seen a situation in which someone had a debt of 120% annual APR. That means this person borrowed $2,600 only to pay $6,000 for this debt over time.

It is in a creditor's or bank's best interests that you don't default on your loans...*not yours*. These days, you can call creditors and ask them to possibly reduce your interest rate. Some companies will, some companies don't, but you should always ask.

Banks can also provide you with "zero percent interest rate" for *X* number of months. Usually it's 18 months, and you can make balance transfers and pay zero percent on that debt. Doing this supports your financial goals. With one of my clients, we called the company and said, "Look, this is a mother of three and her finances are a mess, but she's trying to get back on track. What can you do?" They responded by saying, "We'll freeze her interest rate as long as she is not delinquent on her payment." Instead of getting her out of debt in the four years it normally would've taken, we ended up getting her out of debt in a matter of 11 months!

Work with your creditors. Even if they say no the first time, keep trying. Keep a positive attitude. It's okay if one person says no. Don't cry about it, don't get stressed about it, just say to yourself, "Great. I got one 'no,' but the sooner I get all of those out of the way, the quicker I'll get to a 'yes.'" Don't be afraid to call daily. Ask for the person who can help you do what you're trying to do. You have to take the time and initiative. Don't give up! If you give up after one or two tries, you and your family are the ones who end up paying the price.

Use credit cards that support your goals.

There are some people who know that if they have access to credit, they're going to spend it all. If you're a spender with a $25,000 limit credit card, you're most likely going to max it out. Why not get a prepaid credit card instead? When your paycheck comes in, set yourself straight by getting a prepaid card.

For example, if you spend $300 on gas each month, then get a prepaid credit card and put in $300 of your own money. You're really tricking your mind into thinking you're using a credit card, when in reality it's your own money. When you do that, you're keeping your budget commitment to yourself. And that feels great.

You may get another prepaid card that supports your grocery budget. If you spend $500 to $600 on groceries, then you can put that on a different prepaid card. Why? Because then you know that that's how much you have available to spend, and you'll never go over your budget.

Now that you've set these boundaries for yourself, you'll know that if you spend your prepaid grocery card before the end of the month, you'll have to figure out where the extra cash is going to come from. Maybe you'll have to dip into your entertainment budget for the rest of that month. Limits like these will force you to exercise a little more self-control next time. Remember, the choice is always yours.

Consider getting a new job.

When you know how much net income your family needs, you can also make smarter choices regarding the employer that you work for. For example, I knew someone who needed to bring a monthly net of $3,400 into her household. Her paycheck was $700 short. At this point, it wasn't about the money. It was about worth and value. This woman was very stressed out, knowing that she didn't make enough money. When we looked at her finances, I said, "It's not that you don't have enough. It's that you've chosen the employer who gives you time for money." Examining those things can help you understand how much money your family needs to live a comfortable life.

Pay off your mortgage sooner.

If you want to pay off your mortgage more quickly, send one mortgage payment to your principal at the end of the year. Just one extra payment toward your principal every year can eliminate years of interest and payments from your mortgage. As your principal is reduced, so is the amount of interest you pay. Find a way to save for that extra payment throughout the year or use "found" money like a tax return to make that extra payment toward your principal.

Of course, you could always pay even more toward your principal each year if you can until it becomes *zero*. If your principal is zero, then you no longer have to pay interest either. Just like that, you're living in a debt-free home. Most mortgages have no prepayment penalty. Make sure that's true of yours.

If you're planning to refinance, consider the effect it will have on your long-term goals. When refinancing, most people extend their mortgage payments to pay out for 30 years. Let's say you're on a 20-year mortgage. You have two or three years left to pay. But you want tuition for your kids to go to college, so you refinance your property to do so. Now, you're paying that mortgage for another 10 years. Make sure that's something you're able to do and that you really want to do.

Use time to your advantage if you have a balloon payment.

One thing you have on your side right now is time if you have a balloon payment in several years. And if you have time on your side, that means the amount of money you can build in interest in your accounts can ultimately support you by the time your balloon payment is due.

Let's say you were on the verge of losing your home and the bank offered to modify your loan and create something that supported that mortgage payment based on 35% of your income. In order to do that, the loan likely included a balloon payment at the end. They'll say, "We'll revise your notes and we'll reduce your mortgage payment. We'll make your mortgage payment on 75% of your loan, and here's what's going to happen with the remaining 25%. At the end of the term, you're going to owe us a balloon payment, okay?" Gulp. Okay.

Of course, in between that time, you'll probably end up refinancing. But I like to tell my clients that if they know what the balloon payment is going to be over a period of years, then they should start saving for it now. The balloon payments are not going to come overnight. Be sure to look at that big number seriously. Don't ignore it until it becomes another financial problem.

Some families will say, "Oh, I can afford to pay this," and when I ask them, "What are you doing about your balloon payment?" they say they are doing nothing. Which means that they are just putting it off. They'll either refinance and get into more debt later, or they can start building a plan right now...a plan that could support them in getting out of this balloon payment. That way, by the time that balloon payment is due, they're writing the check for that amount, no problem. And that's because they took action now.

So just like you don't wait until your kids graduate from high school to start planning for college, don't wait until that balloon payment is due to worry about it.

Find ways to create a little more income.

Today there are lots of opportunities to make extra money because of the internet. There are many online gigs...from transcription services to website building...that you can do part-time that allow you to work from home.

Even better, you could prepare a list of your contributions to your employer and ask your boss for a raise. If the answer is "no," ask if a raise might be possible in the near future. Ask if there's anything extra you can do to secure one. You never know what the answer might be until you ask.

Children can help contribute to your family's well-being, too. Get your kids involved with simple business-related tasks like packaging. Your kids could also recycle. Recycling is very big right now. Not only can it help support your household, but it helps support the earth overall. We can always use more of that.

Chapter Five

RETIREMENT PLANNING

Retirement isn't for old people.
Retirement is about continuing to fulfill your life
in the things you want to do.

One woman recently asked for my help and for the first time ever, I had to say, "I can't help you." She looked at me with such despair and asked, "What do you mean?" I had to tell her that, at 70 years of age, I could not support her with her retirement. At this point, it was too late. And so, she knew she'd have to work for the rest of her life. This is more common than most people realize. Unfortunately, a lot of people end up in this situation because they didn't know all the resources that were available to them.

I hope by reading this book, you now know you have the power and the knowledge to impact your financial destiny. Retirement is not when people get old and then they can't work or they don't want to work. Our cultural beliefs are misleading. Retirement really is more of the opportunity to be able to not work as long or as much or at something someone else forces you to do. So, it's all mindset as well as creating the awareness of the resources around you to help you get where you want to be.

There are a few more things I want you to be aware of that impact your retirement...your age and your life circumstances *right now*. Those two things are important factors when planning for retirement.

What's age got to do with it?

Younger people don't really think about retirement at all, let alone as a priority. But someone who's in their 50s or older? Big difference.

On my website, www.evamacias.com, I have different age categories that you can click on to start paying attention to the things to do based on your age today. Let's take a look at each age bracket category.

20 year olds

In my experience, most women in this category don't pay a lot of attention to retirement because they're like, "Oh, that's for my parents." It would be so much better if they were like, "I'm going to be able to put money away in this retirement savings bucket so that potentially I'm able to not work as hard or as long as my parents did." See, different perception.

If you're in your twenties and determine that you don't want to work 'til your 60 but would rather be work-free at 50, and you're going to put in 30 years of service into your career or your own business to make it happen, that is totally doable. But if, instead, you think you'll work for someone, never put a dime away, and then expect the system to sustain you at retirement...well, you'll be in for an unpleasant surprise of relying on meager Social Security checks to come in every month until you die.

30 year olds

I know a lot of 30-year-old women who don't own a savings account. They just don't. They own the checking, but not the savings. I'm like, "Why? Go open up a savings account. You need that more." Once again, it's important that you pay attention early on so that you can have the leverage of saying, "I don't want to work as long."

40 year olds

Once you're in your forties, most people have kids who will graduate high school soon, or maybe they're already off to college or living on their own. Often this is when people have the time and motivation to put money away. The days of choosing between your children's needs over your own are becoming fewer...especially if you've been saving beforehand.

So, when you reach your mid- to late-forties, whatever the case may be, you don't have to choose one or the other anymore when you properly set up a monthly budget and continue with financial planning. You're now able to say, "Yes, of course, I'm going to still be able to maximize my retirement, and I'm also going to be able to give my child money."

Another outcome of being 40-something is that's when people start really paying attention to retirement. So, from

40 to 60 or 65 is when people tend to really get focused on putting additional money away. That age bracket really sets people up to focus on that…not only after your child leaves home, but also beforehand.

50 year olds

Time is of the essence now. Between the age of 50 and 60 you're limited in the amount of time you have left to fund your future. The longer you wait, the more money you need to put away. So, that's why creating urgency when you're young is so important. Don't wait until you're 50 to realize, "Oh yeah, I'm going to retire in about 10 years. It's time to look at this, because now retirement is getting closer."

I see this all the time with clients, especially teachers. I give presentations to teachers quite often and when I do, I usually ask, "Does anybody have less than five years to retire?" Lots of hands go up. Then I say, "Great! Have you already had a review with your pension plan?"

Silence.

Then there's usually someone who says, "Oh, I'm going to do that maybe the year before." That's a big no-no. Do it now. Because you're going to get a really big surprise once you find out that you'll retire with about 50 to 60% of your current income. That's like a 40 to 50% pay cut. "What do you mean, a pay cut?" And then I explain, and we take a look at the formula. Awareness is critical.

Life happens. Now what?

Just like your age bracket, your life circumstances change, too. I received a phone call recently from one of my clients who I met about four years ago. When we first met, she and her husband had a beautiful baby boy. They were in my office to discuss financial planning based on their new and future life together.

But she called to tell me her living situation was changing. As soon as I hear things like that, immediately I think, "They're getting a divorce." And, sadly, I was right. I'm a newlywed as I write this book. I want couples to stay married forever. But the reality is that sometimes that doesn't always happen.

I have another client who is 67 years old and called to discuss the financial ramifications of her upcoming divorce… after 30 years of marriage. That is crazy to me. I would think that after that long they would stay with each other forever, but that doesn't always happen either.

So, it's important to understand how our age and our life circumstances at that age impact our retirement. If you're in your twenties and getting divorced, that's going to be very different than if you're in your fifties and getting a divorce. When you're in your twenties and separating assets, you still have about 40 more years to reboot, so to speak. You have more time to rebuild your assets. But if you're in your fifties, now you're dividing 50% of your assets. That could likely delay your retirement to potentially work another six to 10 years.

It's important to recognize that wherever you fall in the different age brackets *combined* with the different circumstances of life means you have to pay attention to both and make better decisions accordingly. One client of mine was able to work out a deal within her divorce to be able to keep a certain $60,000 investment that was performing well. After they looked at all their assets, she said, "Look, I want to keep this investment for myself. I will pay you out the $60,000 from our assets, rather than having them taken from this particular account." Her awareness of her age and life change made this decision and ultimate deal on her behalf possible.

One of the advantages she had is that she's always been consistent with coming to see me. She made her one-on-one appointments with me throughout the course of her marriage. Any time her financial situation changed, I was the person she called first. She would say, "This is changing. What should I do?" Or, "Hey, I'm thinking about buying a car. This is what I'm going to do." Or, "Hey, I'm thinking about moving out from the West Side to this area. What do you think?" She paid attention to her finances and sought answers when her life circumstances changed in any way.

She took advantage of the resource that I am to her. By doing so, we developed a relationship based on trust and open communication. She knew I would advise her in her best interests, regardless if she were married or single. She knew that, regardless of the circumstances of her life, I wanted her to be in the best situation possible.

Life circumstances can happen in the reverse as well. I meet with single clients who are about to get married. I met with two 24-year-olds who want to get married in five years, and they're opening accounts now. It's my job to inform them that, even though they'll be sharing assets leading up to the marriage, until they are married those accounts belong to them as individuals.

Ask for help.

Shit happens. It is okay to ask questions about what you don't know…especially when it comes to money and your life. It's okay to experience feelings that come up when you're addressing life-changing circumstances. You're human. It is okay to feel sad. It's okay to cry. It's even okay to laugh. Whatever is coming up for you, allow yourself to feel it. Get it out of your system. Don't let feelings manifest into binge-eating or binge-shopping…both of which cost money! Allow yourself to feel your feelings, let them out of your body, and believe that everything's going to be okay.

Evaluate your current employment.

We often think, "My employer gives us great benefits, so I don't have to worry about it." But we don't really know what will happen in the future. What if you're not planning to stay there?

In many cases, employers present you with amazing retirement plans, but you have to know how the formula works. Every retirement plan that an employer provides is based on a formula. Understanding that formula to its fullest will allow you to say, "You know what, it's in my best interests to stay here until I retire," or "I'm going to give X number of years here in order to maximize my benefits." When choosing an employer, understand the benefits and how they'll work for you.

Who wants to go to work every day and think, "I'm only working here for the money?" There has to be some other incentive. If you don't see yourself with this particular employer, that's okay. Many people think they have to depend on their employers to create a retirement plan or to provide insurance and the like. That is just not true. Whether employed or self-employed, you can still be responsible for managing these items.

Anticipate and plan for your earnings "gap" after retirement.

If you anticipate and calculate your drop in earnings after you earn your last paycheck, you can figure out how much money you need to put in to make up the difference. You can use a formula to calculate an exact amount.

Determine how many years of service you will put into your employer. The more you work, the more you get. The average person with a pension receives between 60% and 70% upon retirement. Let's say you started working when you were 30 and now you hope to retire at 60. At the time you started working, you had an annual salary of $32,000. Now, you're 60 years old and you're earning $60,000.

Depending on whether you're on Social Security or on a peer system—whatever your retirement fund is with your employer—you're only going to receive a certain percentage of your salary. Let's say you receive a 60%. How are you going to fill in the additional 40%? That's what we call the retirement drop or gap. And in this case, 60% of $60,000 is $36,000. That takes you back to about the same pay you earned when you started.

Nobody likes to go back to where they started. Knowing the numbers allows you to determine how much you need to save. And, as always, the sooner the better. That way, when you retire, you will already have the remaining 40% put away, whether it's in an IRA or in cash-value life insurances or paying off your home so you can live off of reverse mortgage from the equity of your home. Figure out the number that applies to you.

Know the special circumstances of working for a church, school, or hospital.

There is often a lot of confusion about how employment at a school, church, or hospital affects Social Security income. Clients have told me that they learned at a workshop that they're going to receive 100% of their Social Security and 100% of their retirement funds, whether or not they work for a school, church, or hospital. But, if they look at the back of their Social Security statement, it will actually say that there's a windfall elimination provision.

You'll be receiving your Social Security, but it may not be 100% of the total amount. This affects everyone differently because some people have worked for more years at these organizations and made more money, while others have made less. Know that the windfall elimination provision or the government offset will ultimately create change for you.

Check your statement. Recently, Social Security stopped sending them through the mail in order to go paperless and save trees. So, create an online account. Don't leave it up to them. You are responsible for making sure you are receiving your Social Security statement and are looking over it. Too frequently, people don't even open their statements. Instead, they think, "This doesn't apply to me right now. I don't want to retire yet." On the contrary, now is the time to take a look at them. Now is the time when you can make those changes and determine how potentially receiving two retirement plans can affect you. This is particularly important if you work for schools.

I work with a lot of teachers who have not always been teachers, but have worked in the private sector and contributed to Social Security. Now, they are part of a school system and they're participating in CalSCTRS. It provides retirement, disability, and survivor benefits for full-time and part-time California public school educators. Make sure you know where your money is, what type of retirement account you have, and the impact it has on your Social Security. This way you can ensure your ability to receive two checks, one for Social Security and one for the retirement plan that's offered at the school, church, or hospital.

Plan A or Plan B? Or is it Plan C?

If you don't have a Plan A, you might just end up working the rest of your life. That's Plan B. One of the first questions I always ask my clients is when do they see themselves retiring. Most people say that they've never really thought about it. And my response to that is, "So, do you plan to work for the rest of your life?" Many reply that they wish they could already be done working right now.

You need to be honest with yourself. With Plan B, you'll probably be working until you're 70 or 75. But your health is a major concern and something you should take into consideration. You may not be able to work for as long as you hoped. I had a client who was originally planning to retire at the age of 67. Unfortunately, she suffered a head aneurysm and was forced into retirement at the age of 60. She didn't plan to have an aneurysm…it just happened like many other unexpected events in life. Her plan had been to collect from the two employers she worked for, but even then it wasn't enough in the end.

So, we created a new plan to support her financially. Originally, plan A was to collect these two retirement plans. Plan B was to retire at the age of 67. Neither of those things ended up occurring, so we had to shift things around. In the end, she did collect from both plans after all, but it came in a different form than she'd expected. The new plan, Plan C, meant retiring at 60, reducing her debt, and knowing that she only had a fixed amount of income.

Retirement is supposed to be fun.

Retirement isn't for old people. I know 40-year-olds who are retired. One of my clients is 38 and retired with multiple streams of income. Retirement is meant to be a new chance to continue to fulfill your life in the things that you want to be, do, and have…whether it's traveling, volunteering, pursuing new passions, starting a new business, or moving out to the country. Visualize how you want your retirement to look and follow your plan to get there.

Chapter Six

YOU'VE WORKED HARD FOR YOUR MONEY, MAKE YOUR MONEY WORK HARD FOR YOU

When it comes to money you think of numbers.
But a lot of it is not just the numbers.
It's letters. It's words.

When I first started in the industry, there was a woman who wouldn't meet with me to review her finances. Like many of my clients who are women, she delayed coming to see me out of fear and because she was embarrassed. She thought I might judge her. But like I always tell my clients, "I don't judge. I'm not God. I leave that up to Him."

But one day, five years later, she came to my office and we opened her account. She had $83,000 sitting in a bank account. She said that she probably was receiving a one percent interest rate on those funds. I said, "One percent? You're lucky if you get a tenth of a percent." She asked, "What do you mean?" Just from looking at her account statement, I showed her she had made 55 cents on that $83,000. I literally pulled out a dollar and said, "If I give you this dollar right now, I've made you more money than the bank has."

"What do you mean?" she asked. I asked, "How often do you pay attention?" She said that she honestly just looks at the balance and that's it. That's when I circled the numbers on her statement and said, "I know."

If you have $83,000 sitting in an account somewhere and it made 55 cents, is that your money working hard for you? I don't think so, and I'm guessing you don't either.

If you want to make money work hard for you, you must pay attention to your accounts and allocate them according to the highest return for you based on your financial goals. By shifting that client's $83,000 among her emergency account, a college fund for her granddaughter, and a retirement account, she was now going to make an average of 2.25%. Over the year, $1,800 had been added to her account. That's a lot better than 55 cents.

When you take the time to pay attention, you can make your money work hard for you instead of the other way around. By understanding interest rates, terms, and financial jargon, and then making intentional decisions about where you open accounts and why, you're in control.

I can't tell you how many times I've been asked, "What do you mean?" when discussing the details of my clients' accounts. This chapter is all about telling you what I mean.

Convenience may be costing you money.

Many people open a checking or savings account based on the location of the bank, whether it's close to work or to home. Seriously. One client I worked with chose to open up a CD at a bank near her that paid one percent. She thought her money was "safe" because it was in the bank for five years.

But then I showed her that she was actually in the negative. She asked, "What do you mean?" I showed her that the bank would be deducting a processing fee or a statement fee of $30. That means she now had less than the money she put into the CD five years ago.

Another action of convenience some clients take is to open a savings or checking account where they have their mortgage. But, most banks operate the same way. Having your savings or checking accounts there could be costing you money. Credit unions tend to give slightly better rates than a bank. It just takes time to do some research and find out. When I ask clients what rate they are getting for their checking account, the answer is usually, "I have no idea." Well, it's time to find out. If you're putting your money into an account, what is that account doing for you?

What's the cost of accessibility and convenience? When you go to fast food restaurants, the convenience is awesome, but the price you're paying is that you're putting fuel into your body that isn't quite the best for your system. It's exactly the same thing with money. Just because you're putting it into a bucket that says savings or retirement or college fund doesn't mean that your money's working hard for you.

Don't pay for your own money.

"What do you mean?" I'm like, "They're called fees."

Understand the fees behind everything, from checking accounts to savings accounts to retirement accounts. There are savings accounts that charge you $15 to $30 per month if you don't keep a minimum balance. So, if you don't have enough money, they're going to charge you. If you have enough money, they're not going to charge you. Think about that. How crazy is that? Move the money you do have to a savings account that has no minimum or to one where you have the minimum amount required to avoid those fees.

Let's say you go to the grocery store, use your debit card, and get some cash back. Some banks charge you a fee to get money that belongs to you. Does that make sense? You have an account with a bank with thousands of dollars in it, but you want a quick $100 from an ATM. And the bank where your account is is going to charge you a dollar. It's so funny to me when people are like, "Oh yeah, can I have cash back?" And I'm like, "You just paid a dollar to use your own money." That makes no sense.

Pay attention to the numbers.

Do you know how your 401k works through your employer? When I ask that question, my clients often ask, "What do you mean?" What I mean is, just because your employer provides a 401k doesn't mean it's the best plan for you. Your employer probably has no idea how the plan works either because they're not running the plan, someone else is. Do you know what they're doing with your money?

When we start looking at the numbers, I'm able to show clients that sometimes their plan provides accessibility to their funds, and that costs them money. "What do you mean?"

Well, when you have a 401k and it's invested in mutual funds, you pay the price of that. Because the plan makes it easy for you to borrow a loan against yourself (meaning to get a distribution from the plan, even if you pay taxes on it), you pay for that convenience, even if you don't use it.

Many clients have had their retirement plans fail simply because they didn't pay attention. I had someone putting about $5,000 into a retirement account each year. After looking at her statement I asked, "Do you know how much money you lost this year?" And she said, "What do you mean?" I told her she lost $3,000. And she said, "Oh my God, what do you mean I lost $3,000? I keep putting $5,000 in every year." I explained that she didn't pay attention to the negatives on her statements. The negatives are not identified as "you lost this much money." The negatives are sometimes quoted in parentheses. If you don't know the numbers, you don't know the negatives.

Read the words.

Financial jargon is like a whole different language. We tend to think of finance as money. Or, when we think of money, we think of numbers. The thing is, a lot of it is not numbers. It's letters. It's words.

Pay attention to the details in the words. It's those details that people tend to forget because they don't take the time to read what they're doing.

Invest in good investments, not the stock market.

The majority of people put their money in the stock market. I'm not bashing the stock market. But I 100% believe if you don't understand it, you should not be putting money in the stock market. If you do, you're putting 100% of your funds at risk without understanding the results of what that can create for you. That's why so many people suffered in the economic downturn of 2008. They didn't understand the market. They were relying on others to understand it for them.

I know that many people love to say, "I'm in the stock market," or "It's invested in the stock market." It's just so nice to say that. It sounds prestigious.

Well, I couldn't care less if it's in the stock market or not. It just has to be a good investment. When people lost about 40% of their investments in 2008, I would have rather had my money under my mattress. I would have kept a lot more. That's right, because I wouldn't have lost 40% of my investment.

High risk, high reward is not a true statement. Not every high risk will give you a high reward. It's called high risk for a reason. Because sometimes you risk more than what you're going to be rewarded with.

Benefit yourself.

If your employer doesn't offer you any benefits, figure out what options are available to you elsewhere. If your employer doesn't offer you a 401k, that doesn't mean you can't have one. It means you have to look at different avenues of creating one, such as an IRA, a traditional Roth IRA, or a cash-value life insurance.

For many employers, benefit plans aren't as great as they used to be anyway. We no longer see large pension plans. So, even if they're offering you benefits, be sure to research any alternatives that you could add to your existing plan to help support your family's financial goals.

Know the difference between simple interest and compound interest.

Many people don't understand the difference between simple interest and compound interest, and it's something we learned—or should have learned—at a very young age. There is a huge difference.

Simple interest: Let's imagine you have an account where they've promised to pay you 10% interest. Great! You just earned 10% for the year. Simple.

Compound interest: That's interest on top of interest. This means you've got 10% for the end of the year. But the following year, you're going to get an additional 10% on the 10%. The following year you're going to get 20% on the 20%. It builds up over time, and the value of compound interest can ultimately change your finances drastically.

If you put $250,000 away and compound that over time, you're now talking about an amount that you never even thought was possible. The number is going to be well over a million. Why? Because compound interest has the power to multiply your money. If you saved a penny one day and kept compounding it, you'd be at a million dollars before you knew it. With a compound interest account, your money is going to start working much harder for you.

Maximize your returns with minimum downside.

Look at what happened in 2008—people were living in fear because the market had just crashed. There are plans in the market that don't require you to take that risk. For example, index funds allow you to mirror the market. They're like a copycat of the market.

You might look at what happens in the market and think, "I don't want to risk my money." Risk is the key here. If you're not a risk taker, seek out plans that give you what's called "principal protection." These plans protect your money, they protect your interest, and they protect all the money that you keep putting in there.

Many clients think that sounds too good to be true, but they're not. So, what's the catch? It's very simple. The banks are basically saying, "We'll give you these great plans, but in return you have to sign a contract with us for X number of years." It might be 10 years, it might be 13 or 14, or it might be 16. To put it in plainer terms, you're investing your money with them, and in return they're asking for your time. In this case, the so-called "catch" is that you're committing to them for a matter of 10, 13, 14, 16 years, but in return they're giving you a fantastic plan. They're making sure that your money is always there for you.

Be your own bank.

I meet a lot of families who are very stressed about their debt. I worked with one woman who had $150,000 in a 401k, but she was constantly stressing out about her debt and how she was paying really high interest rates. Finally I asked her, "Have you ever thought about using your own money by pretty much becoming your own bank?" And she said, "What do you mean?" She told me she couldn't touch any of her 401k money because she didn't want to pay any penalties. I said, "No, no, no, no, no. What if you let your money start working for you? What if you took out a loan against your own money and paid off your credit cards?"

She had $35,000 of debt. By taking a loan on her 401k, the payments she made were payments back to herself. Her money could then work much harder for her by paying herself rather than different banks and credit cards with high interest rates.

In other words, she'd be using her own money to create her own bank. By using this system, her monthly payment was actually less than what she was originally paying altogether on a monthly basis. This system made her money work hard for her. It was important for her to remember, however, that she could not, at any time, miss a payment, because defaulting would defeat the whole purpose.

Know the difference between a withdrawal and a loan. As a loan, you're putting this money back. As a withdrawal, you're going to pay penalties if you're not of age, and you're going to pay taxes no matter what. Putting the money back where it came from gives you the leverage of saying, "I don't pay penalties and I don't pay taxes." Your money is working for you.

Manage your credit cards.

People often ask me how many credit cards they should have. How many is too many? I worked with one young woman who owned 26 credit cards. My question was, "Why?" I know other people who think one is more than enough. Frankly, it isn't really a question of how many. The real question is, what can you afford to pay if you're in debt?

Ask yourself, "How much money do I make on a monthly basis?" If you're using 15% of your income, then you can have one credit card or you can maybe have an extra one for emergencies. Maybe you can even have three cards, but not 26. You don't have to apply for a new credit card just because a department store offers it to you. You don't have to get a new card just because the company sent an ad in the mail. Know how many credit cards you can realistically handle on your income.

Get your banks and credit unions to work with your financial plan.

The best way to get your bank or credit union to work with your financial plan is to go in and let them know what your financial goals are. You can always ask them for help when you need it.

Particularly with car loans, if your bank or your credit union offers a lower interest rate, ask them to work with you. Ask them if you can refinance your car, and frequently they'll say yes because they will automatically take the money out of your checking account. Your banks or credit unions might just become your friends by lowering the interest rate that you pay on personal and car loans. As always, do your homework!

Depending on what type of credit card you have, you can go to your credit union or your bank and say, "Look, this is what's going on. What are my options?" One of the things that banks do is offer an introductory, zero percent interest rate on credit cards. This way, you can potentially do balance transfers.

Use balance transfers to get out of debt faster.

As I mentioned above, if your bank or credit union offers zero percent interest rates, it's important to take advantage of that. Frequently, when you consolidate your debt into zero percent interest rates, you end up paying zero interest on the debt. As a result, you're able to send in as much as possible and pay that off in a fixed period of time.

Be mindful of the terms though. Let's say you have $20,000, and your zero percent transfer is for 12 to 18 months. It may be challenging for you to transfer those accounts unless you know you'll be able to pay them off in time.

Create lifetime income.

Lifetime income is a beautiful thing and absolutely possible. Once again, do your homework. There are different types of lifetime income accounts and percentages out there. It's beneficial to have a coach in situations like this because they are better suited to doing the research and setting you up in a plan that will garner you the highest guaranteed lifetime income. In the end, it's kind of like getting two pensions, one you created for yourself by managing your money wisely and another you're receiving through Social Security.

Protect your money.

At the end of the day, protection is making sure your money is going to be there when you need it, whether it's in a retirement plan, a cash-value life insurance plan, or invested in your home. Protection is choosing a plan that will support you and help alleviate risk.

There are many ways you can protect your money. You can protect it by paying attention to your finances and staying vigilant. You can protect it by having insurance. You can also protect your money by making sure that it's always growing for you.

Protect yourself while protecting your parents.

Often, you want to stretch your money enough to be able to care not only for your spouse and children, but for your parents as well. This issue hits home for me personally, as you know. While I don't necessarily take care of my parents financially all the time, I always make sure they're okay.

Let's say you want to give your parents a certain amount of money on a monthly basis. In my case, I sat down with my mother and said, "Mom, I love you. You know I never want you to die, but I know that's something that we need to talk about. You're much older. I may pass before you, but if we're basing this on our ages, you're probably going to go first." So, we had a conversation and I told her, "Look, I know it stresses you out that you might not have set yourself up financially, but if it's okay with you, may I please purchase life insurance so that us kids are not stressed out about where we're going to get this money later?"

That made her cry, and not because she was thinking, "Oh my God, my daughter is thinking about my death." She admitted that it was actually something she'd wanted to do, but she just didn't know how. Even something small like a life insurance plan can help you protect your parents. If they pass before you without making sure their money worked hard for them when they were young, then the whole family is going to live with that unless you do something before that happens.

Look at your monthly expenses. If you can afford to put $50 or $100 a month into life insurance for your parents, it'll be much easier to start now rather than wait until they've passed to worry about their financial affairs. If you invest that money in your parents, you're honestly making your money work harder for you. If you don't, you'll likely need to use your credit cards or get a bank loan to pay for end-of-life expenses.

If you realize you've been spending $100 a month on material items you don't really need, ask yourself why you aren't spending that same amount on something that's so much more valuable, like your parents.

Trust your intuition.

Trust yourself and the choices you're making. Your intuition, especially as a woman, always lets you know what will serve you well. And when you want additional guidance or to weigh other options, seek the help of a financial expert.

There are so many wonderful people out there willing to help you, but there are also people out there who unfortunately only help themselves. When it comes to your money and your finances, trust your intuition. Trust that you're making the right choices with the right people.

There is a lot of information out there, but there's also a lack of wisdom. There are a lot of people claiming that they can help you financially, but trusting them often leads to a horrible experience for some people.

You can choose the person you want to work with. That person isn't chosen for you; you get to choose. Keep an open line of communication between you and your financial adviser, your financial coach, your insurance agent, and/or your banker. Listen to your instincts. Know that the person you can trust most is yourself. I really 100% believe that when you come from there, you'll never go wrong.

Numbers don't lie, only people do.

Once you decide to work with a financial expert, you'll want to make sure you can trust the person who's sitting in front of you to have your best interests at heart. I was interviewed by a woman who said, "You're the fourth financial expert I've interviewed, and I'm going to make a decision based on what each of you has told me." Great. Awesome. I said, "I literally don't care what they told you. I only care what I'm going to tell you and what your goals are."

I believe the reason she chose me is because I asked her fundamental questions involving the well-being of her life in different scenarios. I asked her about her marital status and whether or not she has or would be having children. I asked her if she planned to buy a house. I asked if her money was protected and how. I asked if she knew what would happen if her husband passed before her and vice versa. Mind you, I haven't always been chosen. There have been people who have said, "You know what? The way you say it just doesn't work for me." And I'm okay with that.

But, by asking these questions about her, we began to develop a relationship. I didn't just ask for her numbers and tell her she needed me as her adviser. My approach is more like, "Let me educate you so that this way, if I am your planner and no longer in the picture, you will know what to do next." Developing a relationship with my clients is much better than having them trust me one time and that's it. My goal is to develop value for my clients so that, from that point forward, we continue to build trust throughout the stages of their life.

It's all about you and your finances. That's the end to that conversation. I just happen to be a piece that will support you in supporting your goals. I'm a neutral party to this. You are not. We just need to look at the end result of what you want to create in each new circumstance and then move forward with what's best for you. By developing a relationship with your financial adviser, you are also developing a relationship with your finances.

Know how much a coach will cost if you *don't* have one.

Having a coach will support you in achieving all of your retirement goals. You could end up paying a higher price in the long-run if you *don't* have a financial coach to help you do your homework.

A financial coach's purpose is to give you a neutral perspective on your finances. People can often become emotionally attached to their money, so it's very helpful to have a coach who can be objective and honest. NBA superstar Kobe Bryant may be one of the greatest basketball players of all time, but even he had coaches who helped him get to where he is today. You may not be on the same level as Kobe Bryant, but having a coach will help support you financially in a similar way.

Now, how expensive will a financial coach be? It depends. Some financial coaches are willing to work at no cost as long as you do business with them. Other financial advisers are fee-based, and you get to pay for their expertise. There are other financial coaches who just charge a set fee and in return they give you a blueprint of your finances and send you to the appropriate parties based on your unique financial situation.

Cost will vary depending on the choices you make, but frequently it's relatively inexpensive to hire a financial coach. Deciding which type of coach works best for you is ultimately in your hands

Money is just money. You have to be the one moving it around.

I often deal with women who are very emotional about money. I always tell them that money has no emotion. They're the ones who are projecting their own feelings onto it.

Take a serious look at your finances and take consistent action to place your money where it does the most good for you. For many people, this can be very scary or intimidating. But when you look at your finances, you start seeing how your money can work for you. At the end of the day, taking the time to see this through can ultimately impact your future in ways that you never even thought possible. Then money doesn't control your thoughts. Instead, you're in control. You've built the habit of deciding where your money should go.

Be consistent.

Constant repetition is important. Repetition over time will give you results in life. People will often tell me, "Well, I can afford to pay $400 on my IRA this month, but I may not be able to in December." Putting money away during the holidays can be challenging. That's why it's important to think ahead, anticipate any roadblocks before they happen, and somehow find a way to make the budget work.

I hear this excuse a lot: "I want to save money, but I don't have money." To which I say, "What do you mean you don't have money? You get paid every month. Of course, you have money." It's a matter of shifting it, applying it, and being consistent. Eventually, your persistence will pay off and give you the end result you want to achieve.

Chapter Seven

WHAT'S BEING LATINA GOT TO DO WITH MONEY?

The true gift of money should be the education behind it and the value of how you apply it.

Ladies, it's time to talk. Now that you know everything you need to know about the basics of budgets and the urgency of saving for your future, now let's take a look at some of the issues that are particular to you, my fellow Latinas.

I grew up in a big family with parents who had little education about money. My parents didn't go to school, but it wasn't necessarily because they didn't want to learn. For them, life was all about working. It was about *earning* the dollar, not *learning* about the dollar. This is a common experience in Latin families. As a result, many of us didn't grow up with a strong financial structure, and now we want something better for our kids. That's how it's supposed to be with every generation...a desire to improve ourselves in order to do better for our families and our cultures. This is true whether you're a Latina or not. You can definitely have an impact on the world in a much bigger way by taking on a new responsibility for achieving financial freedom and then role modeling that for your friends and family.

The only "catch" to working the principles in this book is commitment.

Every time something seems too good to be true, Mexicans will say, "Well, what's the catch?" This happens more often than I'd like to admit. It's true in my family. Every time I talk to them about insurance, someone will undoubtedly say, "Well, what's the catch? What's in it for you?" There has to be a catch to everything.

So, here's what I'll tell them: "Look! You put your money away with an insurance company, and the 'catch' is that you're going to be with them for a period of 10 years. So, for the next 10 years, you're committing to putting $400 or $500 away in this particular plan. That's your 'catch.' After the 10 years have passed, you're free to move your money around as you please." This is typical in a retirement plan. The catch is that you've committed for 10 years.

The Latin population in this country is growing and because of our large numbers, we have a lot of influence. By educating ourselves and applying our newfound knowledge, we can impact our community in a much deeper way. It's okay for someone else to make a living. If someone helps raise your awareness, you pay them a fee. It's a return, right? You're not indebted to them. As I said before, some financial coaches won't even charge you a fee! The only thing they ask of you in return is to do business with them…to commit. The situation is a win-win. In times like these, the "catch" might be a positive thing.

MONEY AND LATIN CULTURE

Big families and big family responsibilities.

Latin families are often very large—there might be as many as eight to 10 kids in a family—so it can be very challenging to save money. I'm not saying it's right or wrong to have a big family. If you're able to afford the expenses and want lots of kids, then by all means, keep doing what you're doing.

On the other hand, as traditional as it might be to have a large family, sometimes we might want to reconsider that number. Just because you grew up in a large family, doesn't mean you also need to have a large family once you get married and have children of your own. The way I was raised was very different from the way my oldest brother was raised. Growing up, he didn't have the freedom to do the things that I did. He was responsible for making sure that his little sisters were okay. He was expected to be the man of the house when Dad wasn't around. And the demands of providing for a family of 10 is very demanding, so Dad wasn't around a lot. It's difficult and expensive to raise a family that way these days.

Helping to support your parents financially while still saving for yourself is another concern for adult Latin children. Finding a way to balance these two needs can be challenging. You might want to consider getting an insurance plan for your parents as your way of supporting them, as we discussed in Chapter Six. I'll bet your parents wanted to put money away for their retirement, but for whatever read they were unable to. Have a conversation with your parents as well as your siblings about pitching in to provide this protection to your parents. Realize that you may not be able give them a fixed amount of money each month, but together with your siblings you can definitely support your parents if, God forbid, something happens to them. Your parents won't have to leave that financial burden to the children because the insurance will be there.

Your parents will feel supported. Your family members get to contribute to the family's well-being. It's a win-win. Over time, there will be less financial responsibility because now you know that insurance is in place in case of emergency. It will be worth it in the end.

Cundinas.

As you know, a *cundina* is very common in Latin culture. It operates like a Mexican or Latin lottery. First you get a group of people together. Each person promises to put away $100 a week, which comes out to $400 a month. If you multiply that amount by the number of people participating, that's how much is being collected on a monthly basis. After that, each person is assigned a number. If you have 10 people in the group, you get a number from 1 to 10. If you're the lucky winner of the draw, you'll be collecting the total sum of money that month. The next month, someone else will get a shot. Think of it as a cash advance.

The key to a successful *cundina* is making sure that everyone is involved and participating. You have to trust that the other people in the group are doing their part. If everything goes smoothly, a *cundina* can help quell your money woes. If it doesn't, it can sometimes be a nightmare.

Imagine trusting 10 people you don't actually know to pay out their portion of the pie every week. What if, for whatever reason, one of those 10 people experiences an emergency and is no longer able to contribute? Then what happens? Realistically, you'll no longer be getting the amount of money that you were putting in. It becomes like a mutual fund that isn't paying out the way you were expecting it to pay out. As I said, there is no contract. *Cundinas* are all based on trust. Make sure you know whom you're doing business with because otherwise you could lose out.

When you trust a financial coach instead of strangers in a *cundina*, you know you're working with someone who has a verified financial background and whose job it is to help people with their finances. In the case of a *cundina*, what you're basically doing is putting your money into the hands of people just like you. *Cundinas* don't normally pay any interest. If you put in $5,000, then you get $5,000. But you don't receive any interest for giving your money to these other people. You're basically saying, "Here's my money for the month. By putting in my money, I'll eventually get everybody else's money." That's definitely a big risk. I talked earlier about minimizing risk.

Most of these *cundinas* just operate on a numbers system. It's not like you're signing a contract. If you're giving someone your cash, you're hoping that they're ethical and moral and that they're going to pay out the way they're supposed to. That's an expensive price to pay for hope.

Cash.

Most people who get paid cash and/or "under the table" don't like to talk about it, but the conversation is necessary. You may be getting quick cash now and thinking, "Wow! This is great! I get cash. I don't have to pay taxes on it." But know how this behavior will impact your future. If you're receiving cash and not paying taxes on it, you may very well end up with nothing in the end.

Nobody wants to pay taxes, but everybody should. Additionally, if you're getting cash but not reporting it, you're also not contributing to your own Social Security. If you do have valid Social Security but your income isn't being applied, you're also reducing the amount of money you'll be receiving at the time of retirement through Social Security.

You may have heard the saying, "Cash is king." But cash can be very hard to keep track of. I know people who get paid cash but don't have a system in place for tracking it. They just say, "Oh! I think I got paid this much," or "I get about this much," because they're not receiving a paycheck, and they never see the numbers in writing.

I read about a study once where the researchers learned that for people who earn cash, it actually hurts a little more when they spend it. I don't know if this has happened to you, but I know it's happened to me. Often, I don't want to break a hundred-dollar bill because I know I'll spend it. Right?

Try to apply the following concept as you would if you were getting a paycheck. Deposit that bill into a savings account and set yourself on automatic instead. Know when your cash deposits are going to take place. If you do get cash, talk to a CPA who can advise you on how to report it. It's important that you're always ethical about your finances.

Immigration.

With immigration being such a hot-button topic—especially in our Latin culture—it's important for everyone to know what a Tax Identification Number (TIN) is and how it can be used to your benefit. I have known many people in the Latin community who are not U.S. citizens or residents but who want to be able to protect their family with retirement plans and life insurance. At the end of the day, they're not able to get the same benefits as citizens.

What you may not know is, as long as you have the required TIN, some insurance companies will give you a life insurance policy. If you have a Social Security Number that was given to you for work purposes only, you can also apply for a similar benefit as if you were a resident or a U.S. citizen.

There's so much immigration reform being considered right now. So many people out there want the opportunity to finally become U.S. residents and citizens. Your immigration status is always changing, so make sure you know where you are now. Ultimately, by filing for Social Security, you can apply for any type of residency here in the United States and qualify for some of these insurance plans and retirement accounts.

If you have only a TIN number, don't get discouraged. Work with a financial coach and try to seek out suitable insurance companies who are offering plans to people who have this Tax Identification Number.

A lot of Latin families will come to the United States from Mexico, earn money through work, and then take that money back to Mexico. If you're living here in the United States, especially in California where we have such a melting pot of people, it's important to apply that money here and to pay your taxes here, so that money can start working back into the economy. The Latin community used to be a minority, but we are growing in numbers and our actions influence the rest of the country. We must do our part in supporting the economy where we work and live.

I encourage people to fix their papers and get your Social Security. It may be a lengthy process, but in the end, the hassle is worth it. If you don't go through it, you'll end up like most of the older generation who've had to move back to Mexico to retire. The ones I know personally are in their seventies, and they're either still working or they're relying on their kids who live here in the States to send them money. Immigration definitely plays a key role when it comes to money in the Latin community.

God.

When I was growing up, my Mom would always say, "*Si, Dios quiere.*" It means, "If God wants it." And my younger self would always ask her, "But Mom, why would God not want it? He must already want it or else He wouldn't put it in front of me."

You might say, "I hope I win the lotto, I hope I win the lotto." But you never buy a ticket. So, it's not going to happen. If you want all of your financial planning to work for you, if you want all of these habits so you can be prosperous in your life, know that God already equipped you with the capabilities you need to make it happen and you must do your part. Buy the damn ticket!

You need to take action and make a commitment to your financial well-being. You have to tell yourself, "I have faith and I trust that all of the choices I'm making for my family are serving my family." Growing up, faith was a big part of my family. It's great that we leave it all up to God, but I'm sure God also wants us to handle ourselves responsibly. I still remember hearing my mom say, "*Si, Dios quiere*" during my childhood, and to this day, I always tease her about it. I say, "He does want it, so what are you doing about it?"

I was raised Catholic, but as I got older I realized that we weren't the only ones. Every time I walked into the household of a Latin family, I would see saints everywhere. You can tell someone is Catholic just by walking into his or her house. Even before you go in—outside, there are the signs. As I've matured over time, I've had these beautiful conversations with my mom. I always tell her, "MOM, it just doesn't make sense to me. If we have so much faith in God that we have saints hanging all around us, why are we constantly forgetting how much He really believes in us, and how He created us with this capability to have amazing relationships with our money?"

In the past, I've told this to my clients when they say things like, "I don't know if I can do it." There's really no point in having all of these saints in your house if you're not going to believe that God put you in the financial place that He did. There's a reason behind it. If you're not where you want to be financially, you're responsible for that. Also, surrender to the fact that this may be part of the lesson that God wants you to learn.

God whispers in your ear but when you don't listen, He screams.

I never really understood what that meant, especially when I was going through a huge financial struggle. It didn't make sense to me. At that time, it was just words on a piece of paper that held no meaning for me. But when I really reflected on them, I realized, "Wow, if I'd never been given this lesson— not just the struggle itself, that's secondary—I probably would not be writing this book right now. No, not probably; I wouldn't be writing this book at all, and you wouldn't be reading it."

But I paid attention to the lesson in my struggles. I believed that God was leading me in a way that I didn't even understand at the time. I just knew that He loved me enough to teach me that lesson. I knew that in order for me to have an impact on others, I needed to step out of my comfort zone and apply what I'd learned to myself before I could source that out to others. If you're going live in a house crowded with all these saints, you need to believe that you can do it. Believe that you're capable. Believe that He wants nothing but the best for you.

Guilt.

A lot of my clients are Latin women, and I can often see that guilt is eating them up inside because they have financial resources. Everybody carries guilt very differently. There's the guilt of, "This isn't what life is supposed to look like for me." Our Latin culture has created these expectations and stereotypes for women: I'm supposed to get married, have a family, raise kids, and that's my life. I have to find a husband or I'm not good enough. I'm not good enough to create a wealthy living for myself.

Guilt is rampant among these women, and the fact is, there's nothing to be guilty about. These are just phantoms that we create in our mind. Your parents never said, "I want you to grow up and feel guilty about money." They wouldn't want that for you. That was something we made up in our heads as a reaction to not having enough money growing up. The guilt can take different forms for everybody.

It's not uncommon for a Latin woman to earn more than her man. And it takes a very confident man who can say, "Yeah, my wife works very hard for what she has." In the past, men were supposed to be the bread winners while the women stayed home. But that has changed. Societal norms have evolved so much. In nearly every household nowadays, both the husband and the wife have to work in order to support the household. Women then feel guilty for going to work and leaving their kids at home. I hear it all the time: "I wish I could stay with my daughters instead of going to work." Those are choices that you get to make.

With men, guilt is not a conversation they have often, if at all. And ladies, I think it's time for us to snap out of that mentality because guilt is not serving us. Guilt is not moving us forward. To do so, we must reject the current position that we're in. Sitting in your shit won't serve you either. If you acknowledge what you're feeling, then slowly you work through it and move on.

I was once told that feelings are like flatulence. They come and go. It's so true. That feeling of guilt might just be there in the present moment. But it too will pass. Be aware and honest. Recognize the feeling when it comes. Say, "Oh, I'm feeling guilty right now." Check yourself: "I don't need to feel guilty because I'm doing something that supports my family. I'm doing something that allows me to love myself."

LET'S CHANGE THE CULTURE

Create a life worth living.

When you give financial peace of mind to yourself and your family, what form does it take? What does it look like? At the end of the day, it's those smiles that come without the shadow of a worry. It's the bright, beautiful eyes of your kids looking up at you and up to you. You'll never be able to buy those things with money.

But when you're calm and fully present with your family, conversations about money become secondary. The more you give—I don't just mean financially, I also mean the more you give of yourself—the less you must work in the morning. You get to spend time with your family instead. What a blessing! It's unfortunate that these days, both mom and dad have to go out and work such long hours. The kids end up spending most of their time with the babysitter. What if it didn't work that way? What if you could create a life where you're off work at three, where you pick up your kids from school, and everyone is sitting at the kitchen table having dinner and conversing at five o'clock? That would truly be a beautiful thing.

In a lot of families I work with, the wife will say, "Oh, no, my husband works nights. I work days, and I actually don't see him until the weekend." That arrangement definitely creates a huge strain in any relationship. So, create a life worth living. Conjure a vision of where you'd like you and your family to be and see if you can't make it reality.

Ask yourself, what do you value most? Do you value family? Do you want to stay home? Do you want to live in a smaller house? Do you want to send the kids to public school instead of private school? Do you want to pay off your debt before you start a family? Do you want to stay single? Those are the financial goals that you need to figure out for you and your family.

The ability to give awareness and knowledge to those who need it is a great gift. But it's also a beautiful thing to give others your time and your money because you're able to experience something that's—well, you can't even put that feeling into words.

Pay attention to where your money goes.

In many of the budgets that I have seen in the past seven years, the majority of expenses are going toward food and drinks. This is particularly true in the Latin community. Over this time, I've come to realize that so many people are in denial about how much of their income is being used on food and drinks.

If you're buying groceries on a monthly basis, and you've given yourself a budget of $600 but you're also spending another $600 on eating out, and then maybe you treat for $200 of drinks afterward, the numbers add up quickly. I worked with a couple who was spending $1,200 on groceries and almost $800 on eating out. It was an unfortunate situation. I got a glimpse of their lifestyle, and I immediately saw why things weren't working out for them. The whole family was in denial about their finances.

Frequently we're spending that kind of money instead of simply saying, "Okay, we're going to take a step back and work on a budget that the family can afford." If you're going to eat out, you might decide to do it on Fridays only, or just once on the weekend.

Food is a part of the other living expenses bucket. It also includes eating out, entertainment, and clothing—you can definitely put about 20% to 25% of your income into this particular bucket. But it's also important to control yourself here. I've seen that other living expenses can sometimes get bent out of proportion when they aren't being monitored carefully. It's easy to go to the grocery store—especially when you're hungry and you're impulse buying and then realize, "Oh my God, I'm so tired and I don't even want to cook. I just want to put the groceries away, but on the way, let's stop and get something to eat."

That's very common. So, set a food budget and stick to it, no excuses. As I discussed earlier, a prepaid credit card can help immensely. If it's $500 that your family needs for food and groceries, then add $500 to that prepaid card. Once you spend it all, it's gone. You'll learn how to better manage your money this way.

Pay your taxes.

Pay your taxes now, so that later on you don't have to deal with the IRS. That's definitely something we all hope to avoid.

Maximize your money.

Make sure that you're spending your cash wisely and that you're also supplementing with those other benefits such as Social Security or 401ks or those extra benefits that most employers provide. Definitely make sure you look into Roth IRAs and cash-value life insurances because both are post-tax.

If you get paid cash, you need to figure out what your options are in regard to investing post-tax...meaning, after taxes. If you're earning cash, you receive a salary reduction form, which is like a 401k. You're not able to contribute to Social Security. You're just getting cash. Options available to you might include Roth IRAs, where you can put your money, or cash-value life insurances. You can still apply for those because they come out of your checking account, and you're actually able to pay for these accounts.

You can still have a 401k, though that might not be what it's called. 401ks are used for the credit factor. However, you can get very similar plans that work like a 401k, such as a traditional IRA. These are pre-tax contributions, and you're allowed to contribute $5,500 a year. Also, if you're over 50 years old, you can contribute $6,500, so be sure to take note if that applies to you. While you may not have the 401k, you can put your money into this similar account. This way you'll ensure your money is protected and that you're working toward your retirement goals.

In order to maximize the cash you have to work for you, you need to make sure that you're making the right choices and implementing portions of cash to an account that can ultimately support you and your financial goals. When you make cash, you can either spend it all and have nothing left at the end of the day, or you can experience the pride of saying, "I saved that, and now it's grown into something more."

Maximize your credit.

I am a big believer that cash is a better alternative to credit cards. If you can live without a credit card, that would be great. But at the same time, we also need credit to buy a house or get a car. Because of that, it's important to establish a good relationship with your credit. At the same time, if you can afford to pay for something in cash, then why not do it?

If you are going to charge your credit card, make sure that you're paying them off at the end of the month because that will still allow you to have credit reporting with the agencies. You'll know that your credit cards are at zero balance every single month, so you won't start feeling the stress of constantly thinking, "Oh my God, I didn't send that payment," or "Now I'm paying this really high interest rate on a pair of shoes that I really don't like, and I think I already gave them away."

Know that you can use both cash and credit cards to your advantage when planning your finances. But, if you can afford to pay for something in cash, then pay in cash.

Know the true gift of money is in education about its value.

I didn't grow up with a lot of money, but I always felt like we had very good friends around us. We didn't expect Christmas gifts during Christmas because we understood that the holidays were really about getting together and enjoying each other's company.

The true gift of money should be the education behind it and the value of how you apply it. Let's say we have two people, and one of them has really bad money habits while the other one has good values in general. You give both the same amount of money. Most likely, the person with the better values will be able to keep that money while the other person will most likely end up losing it.

At the end of the day, know that money is still just a piece of paper. It doesn't control how you wake up, how you feel in the morning, whether you should be happy, or whether you should be sad. When it comes to money, your self-control is what can ultimately give you a life of abundant joy with your family and your friends, a life of peace and faith. If you do it, other people can as well.

Don't assume the worst about the wealthy.

Unfortunately, in our Latin culture, when people are doing very well financially, some people will automatically assume it must be drug money. Let me tell you: I have had the pleasure of meeting a lot of very wealthy families. The reason they're wealthy is because they understand the value of hard work and the value of a dollar.

No matter what your parents taught you, be aware that over time, your kids are also learning from you. If you're doing well, great! There are many, many wealthy people whose families have established businesses and now they have a legacy that they're leaving behind. The parents might have passed on and now the kids own it.

You should never think, "Oh, it must be drug money." No, it's called hard work, it's called dedication, it's called understanding the value of commitment and respect. These are all things that result in money, but also have inherent value in and of themselves. At the end of the day, it's about having good values. Set a good example for your family.

Don't make faith your only financial plan.

Faith should instill confidence in you to take action about money on your own behalf, but it shouldn't be your only plan. Whether the struggle you're experiencing is financial or emotional, know that it's temporary. It *is* temporary. Everything in life, every lesson learned, will always be temporary because we're constantly evolving. We're constantly changing and transforming into different people. I'm not the same person that I was 10 years ago, not even close. Now when I go visit my mom and I see all the *santos* on the walls, I find them beautiful. I embrace them. Ultimately, I really do.

Believe in yourself.

At times, religion can be a touchy subject, just like politics, money, and sex. But even if you don't hold the same beliefs as I do, you can always believe in yourself. Believe in the fact that money is secondary when you're aligned with your god, whichever god you might pray to. As long as your faith feels great in your body and you're helping others, what you're doing is serving a much higher purpose. It's only a matter of time before you start seeing those seeds you planted start to grow and flourish into amazing relationships: a relationship with yourself, a relationship with your family, a relationship with your finances, a relationship with your food.

T. Harv Eker, a renowned money expert, says, "The way you do anything is the way you do everything." There is so much truth to it. If your relationship with your spouse isn't the greatest, all your other relationships most likely aren't that great either. Every now and then, take the moment to reflect and ask God for guidance because He'll always put you on the right path, at the right place, and with the right people, whether it's to learn the lesson or give the lesson. I feel very blessed to have been raised in a family where there was a constant reminder of God.

Love yourself first.

It's important for you to give to others. It's great to want to take care of your family, but you need to take care of yourself first. If you're sick or if you're broke, you won't be able to give your kids anything. Know that you need to fill your cups first, and that's okay. Don't feel guilty about it. Remembering this will support your family in all aspects of life.

Chapter Eight

COMMUNICATING ABOUT MONEY WITH YOUR PARTNER

Communicating about money is like talking about love.
It opens us up to being vulnerable.

Being vulnerable runs counter to being a powerful independent woman, or so we've been told. But that's just bullshit. When it comes to a partnership and money, the biggest gift you can offer is your own vulnerability. I've had many, many married women as clients who tell me they don't want their fiancés or their husbands to know about their finances. Why? Because they're afraid.

So, I'll start by telling you about mine...not so long ago.

I used to be a financial mess with a lot of financial baggage. In the past, I didn't communicate with anyone about money. I also didn't ask any questions. I spent more money than I made. My FICO score sucked. I almost lost my house. I just let it all be, which became more problems. And I was afraid to tell my fiancé. I resisted talking with him because I was like, "Oh my God, what is he going to say? How am I going to approach this? He is going to judge me." I mean, I was already judging myself and operating from an unhealthy place of fear.

But I didn't want to start my marriage with financial secrets. I wanted to have an open, honest, vulnerable conversation…not only for our marriage, but to be truthful with myself. When I was in my financial nightmare, I did not love myself enough to be able to see a much bigger picture and change my path. I wanted him to know that my mistakes led me to where I am today. I wanted him to know that my mistakes are why I now own my financial services company.

I guess my courage to be vulnerable turned out all right. We've been married three months as I write this book.

So now let's take a look at what I've learned after meeting with countless women who are either about to get married or already are.

BEFORE MARRIAGE

Talk about money before you get married.

When you're engaged, you experience so many emotions. You feel so good all the time. Usually your biggest concern about money is how to buy the perfect dress and how to afford the perfect wedding. But, have you asked your partner, "What does your credit score look like?"

Have logical conversations, not just romantic ones.

Are you going to say, "I love you less because you have messed up credit or because you don't have a FICO score of at least 720?" It's doubtful (but if it does lead to that, better to find out now rather than later).

When getting married to someone, you are absolutely making a financial commitment along with your wedding vows. So, before you walk down the aisle, sit down with your partner, and ask each other the following questions:

- How much is your net income?
- Do you have any benefits?
- How much is your debt?
- How do you manage your money?
- What are your financial goals?
- What are our financial goals?
- How will we each contribute?
- Do you want to buy a house?
- What are your monthly expenses?
- Which accounts should we combine, and which should we keep separate?
- What are your desires for retirement?
- Have you done any saving for retirement?

It is critical to your well-being to understanding that whatever your partner financially does or doesn't do is going to impact you.

My husband and I now operate as a "unit." We make financial decisions that are based on what's best for both of us, not just one of us. We come from "we," not "he" or "me."

AFTER MARRIAGE

You must have a marriage plan, just like you operate from a business plan.

When running a business, most people create a business plan, file their taxes, meet with CPAs, pay attention to the bookkeeping. All that you do in a business, but what about in a partnership with the husband and wife? It is common to hear from newly married women, "I'm really married. I'm going to change my name. I've got to order my I.D. I've got to send in all these documents to make sure my new name's on there." Really? You take time to change your name, but do you take the time to say, "Okay, now that we're married, what documents do we need to create? What goals are we going to pursue?"

Relationships are about intimacy.

Intimacy is "into me you see." So, if it's into me you see, that means your partner sees your fear and your vulnerabilities, and you see his. Intimacy means you're operating as one. It's no longer about what does he have or what do I have. It's about what do we have and what do we want to create.

It doesn't matter who *runs* the finances. It matters that both partners are *involved* in the finances.

When couples come to my office, I find out that one person always runs the household finances. Whether you're male and female or a same-sex couple...someone is always in charge. But that doesn't matter as much as being involved in the finances. Both of you. I say that because I have had multiple clients who have no idea what their spouse has in the bank or in debt. They have no idea. Often women will say, "Oh, that's my husband." And I say, "No, that's yours too." There is no such thing as operating as your husband's and yours when it comes to your household finances. You must operate from "we." And you can't do that if you don't know what's going on or you're not working together at your goals.

For example, I have a married client who is 49 years old. She wants to buy a house. And by she, I mean she and only she. Financially she cannot afford to buy a home. She doesn't make enough income. Once she came to see me, she said, "I want to buy a house, so I'm working on my debt." I said, "That's great, but your husband needs to be involved with this as well because he's actually the primary breadwinner." And she said, "Yeah but he has all this debt, and he doesn't want to pay it off." I said, "Okay, right there, there's a huge disconnect. If you and he do not operate from one, it's going to be very hard for you to buy a home. What are you going to do, say, 'Oh, this is my house, not yours'?"

This is crazy to me, but I have another couple who are clients who are in their seventies. She is a retired school teacher. They have a net worth a little bit over $7 million, and she has no idea how to write a check.

Don't put your head in the sand.

If your husband is running your household, women tend to take the easy way out and say, "My husband takes care of that." I will then say, "Don't you think he wants you to be involved in at least knowing? Not only for your part, but maybe your husband needs a little bit of support." By not confronting your finances with real communication and understanding, maybe you keep spending, spending, spending, or vice-versa, but you have no idea what's really going on. Maybe you don't know that your husband just racked up $50,000 of debt because you keep spending it. He keeps borrowing money to pay off your spending habits. That hardly seems fair.

Don't wait until you want a divorce to find out about your finances.

A client of mine in her forties was going through a divorce and she said, "I have never run my household." That divorce caused such an awareness within herself that she immediately learned about how to take care of herself. She started contributing to her retirement fund at work. She signed up for the 401k match program. She started saving money at the bank. Her divorce created urgency and interest in taking charge of her financial well-being.

When you buy a home, you buy responsibility.

If you're ready to save up for a house, figure out together what that looks like. Determine how you each get to contribute to it.

Make a plan to save for your down payment. Figure out how much you can afford to pay for a house.

But be sure to understand, when people want to buy houses, they are actually buying responsibility. When you buy these responsibilities, and if one of the partners is gone, you're now 100% owner of that responsibility. How are they going to make that happen?

In the Latin culture, I see very often that when a husband and wife buy a home, the title is often put in the husband's name. Let's say we're talking about the older generation, where the wife usually stays at home and the husband goes to work. The wife is perceived as maybe not contributing *financially* to the household, and that's why the title might only have the husband's name. But, what happens if that husband passes away? You may rightly think, "It's my husband. This is my house. I've lived here for 25 years. This house belongs to me." Unfortunately, that's not how the state will look at it. The legal system has no idea whether you and your husband had a good relationship. How do they know that he wanted to leave you this property?

Unfortunately, relationships can be lost due to death or they can be broken through financial stresses. Understanding this component of responsibility for protecting yourself and your home is imperative. If you're a wife, and your husband is the only one on the title, address it immediately. Get your name on the title. Set both partners up with a trust. Have the intimate conversation it will take to do so. If a trust costs $2,000, and that's unaffordable for you, decide together how to create that money or how you can adjust your budget in order to make it a top priority for the both of you.

Before my husband and I were married, we bought a home. As our escrow was closing on the new house, I was also closing on selling my old house. But, realistically speaking, I could die within that time of escrow. So, out of my love for him and my responsibility to the new house, I wondered things like, "Where would he get this money for the new house if my house, say, didn't sell?"

Because I took my responsibility so seriously, I looked at my finances and insurances. I had a life insurance policy. I asked myself, "If I were to pass before these escrows close, how much money would I owe him?" I literally did the math, called him up, and said, "Hey, from here until my escrow closes at the other property, I'm just letting you know that you're 22% owner of my life insurance policy. So, if something happens to me before any of this happens, you're 22% owner of my life insurance policy. So, you'll get your money back for my share of the house.

Love builds trust. Trust means responsibility.

Think about it. As an engaged couple, we were relating from one already. So, if I'm getting married to him, and I want the best for him, why would I not want the best for him even if I passed away?

So, my name is on the title of the house I'm selling, and I'm listed as a single woman. Immediately after my escrow closed, I contacted my trust attorney and said, "I need to update my trust. I no longer have the property that I had before. I have this property with my fiancé now." However, the way I had my trust beforehand was that if I passed, 100% of the proceeds would go to my parents. My sister would manage it, sell the house, and give the proceeds to my parents to split 50/50. My life insurance policy takes care of all my eight brothers and sisters, my 13 nieces and nephews, and my dog. I set it up this way. And people think I'm crazy.

Death costs money.

It may sound crazy, but when you die there is a personal and financial burden for others. Think about it. When you die, someone needs to be responsible for your pet. It takes money to do that. Your beloved dog or cat needs food and maintenance. They need care. If someone you trust can't afford it, they're not going to be able to take care of your animal, you know? I can only imagine your children and the financial burden that could cause if you're not protecting them.

Unconditional love means I'm going to love you while I'm here and when I'm not.

So, as soon as I got married, I let the trust attorney know. I said, "By the way, now if something happens to me, 100% of this property goes to my husband, not my parents." I upped my life insurance so that my parents, under all given circumstances, are always taken care of.

It took a few conversations with my trust attorney, and a few hundred dollars to update. I would rather pay a few hundred dollars and update everything to have the peace of mind in knowing that, in any given situation, no matter what, if I pass, everything and everyone is taken care of. That's what love looks like.

Not so much with many of my friends and family. I heard things like, "You guys aren't even married, why would you leave him money?" I said, "But I'm not leaving him money. I'm being responsible for my share of responsibility." I don't know if tomorrow I'll be here. So being in love means being responsible. I love him enough, I care about him enough to leave him better than I found him. I only have the power to do that while I'm alive.

I'd also hear things like, "Wow, you have a few policies. Don't you fear that your money is going to be left to the future wife if something happens to you?" Guess what? I don't care. These are real conversations that I've heard. I'm like, "He's going to be my spouse and when I'm gone, do you really believe that he will stop living if I always loved him and took care of him?" I said, "There's always going to be that little void that if he finds someone to love him and I just happen to financially be able to fund that love, while I'm no longer on this Earth, I will 100% believe that that is just unconditional love."

It's very hard sometimes for women and parents to wrap their heads around that. I think it's hard for us to not think, "If it's not for me, then it's not for anybody else that comes after me." But my belief is, I'm gone. There's a reason why

I'm gone. Just because I'm gone does not mean that he's not going to miss me or vice versa. And it also doesn't mean that I cannot take care of him.

The knowledge that I can take care of him or he can take care of me after one of us dies means it will give us more mental space to grieve and go through our process without having to worry about money.

I've had many women clients who've told me, "I don't want anything to do with him and his life after me." How awful. I'm like, "Why are you still married to him?"

Never allow your financial beginnings determine who you're going to be.

As you know, my parents didn't talk about money or show love in the form I talked about above. They just worked their asses off. I learned a lot from what they were doing to support a family. I also learned a lot from what they were not doing.

After my Mom's sixth child, she went back to work outside the home. I learned that my Dad was somewhat selfish in saying, "I'm just going to retire at 62, whether you guys can afford to pay the house or not. I don't care. Because there's enough children to contribute to it." That was a very traditional mindset with poverty-level surroundings. And that is not the marriage or the life I intended to repeat. I knew that if I wanted an abundance of love, communication, relationship, everything, I need to be that first, before I can expect it from my partner.

Let go of Miss Independence.

My husband wanted to save money and combine our cell phone plans. I started thinking some crazy things. I don't know about all you other ladies, but I know how crazy I can be sometimes. It's not me, it's my ego that's crazy. I was like, "Wait a minute, here I am, this independent woman who has it all together and has her own business, but my husband is going to control my cell phone. I know I want to save money, but I'm supposed to be independent. I'm supposed to have my own thing."

My biggest fear was that I was going to be limited to my independence and my freedom. I seriously had a few days of just having this stupid conversation with myself. Then I realized, wait a minute. I'm married. I want my marriage to last forever, but if it doesn't, all that would mean as far as my cell phone goes is that I would get another provider. I can keep the same number. What's the big deal, here? It was because my fear instantly kicked in. It was like, no I'm afraid. I'm afraid he's going to control. He's not controlling anything. He has your cell phone bill, that is it.

He has no time to look at who I'm calling or not calling. What are you afraid of? It's not like I'm making phone calls to ex-boyfriends at 2:00 o'clock in the morning, you know? It's like what's the big deal here? So, I went into the T mobile store and handled it. I called my husband and said, "Hey they said that if we up your plan to this, it's much better for both of us. Are you okay with that?" He's like, "Yeah, do

whatever you feel is best. You have full access to my account."
I thought, "Wow. That was easy." When you come from love
instead of fear, love will be given. And if it's not, then maybe
you happened to marry the wrong one.

Handle the money talks. Eliminate that stress. Show up as a partner.

If you can attack one of the largest stress factors for couples...
which is money...then everything else is just you being a
human being with your partner.

I remember telling my sister this when her marriage just
seemed like it was being tested financially and emotionally. I
said, "Money should not be the important factor. It should be
creating a closer, more loving open relationship between you
guys. If you come from that, you can deal with the money
matters." However it is that your marriage is being tested,
it's understanding and going back to the why. Why did you
marry this person? Why not love yourself and love him like
you want to be loved? I know it can be hard. I'm a newlywed,
but I know my husband can get on my nerves. I already know
that for a fact.

Practice your appreciation more than your ego.

After moving into our new house together, our neighborhood
had recently experienced some break-ins. So, I went into,
"Oh my gosh, I don't like the location of the house. I like the
view, and I love that we created a new home, but it's too dark
here." I went into fear.

My husband thought I didn't like the house anymore. I told him, "No, I love our house, but there's certain sections that because we're up on a hill it's really dark. We need to find a way to put a light there. I'm just like freaking out." The next morning, he said, "I just want to let you know that the alarm system is going up this morning, and the lights are already in the process of being put up. The alarms will be up and going soon."

After he said that he left, and I jumped in the shower. What started coming up for me was how my thoughts were all about fear…of robbery and burglary. I made it all about that. But he has been working his ass off to get this place to what it looks like now. And now on top of that, he's making it a safe space, where not only has he thought about sensor lights, he's also putting lights in areas that I never even had imagined. And on top of that, he's adding a camera where I can control what I can do with the sensors.

I was much more focused on this idiot of a person who broke into a home versus what an amazing husband I have to create a safe space for me. I jumped out of the shower and called him to say, "You know what, I know this happened in the neighborhood, but everything you're doing I know is creating a safe space. I know that you and I are going to be safe because of all of your hard work." I went from fear to gratitude, just like that. I thought, "You know I couldn't care less if you're not rubbing my feet, honey, but if you're setting me up this way, you love me."

It's easier to point the finger than it is to take responsibility.

It's very rare that I know of a husband and wife who speak about their finances on a monthly basis. Couples don't talk about it. They think the less they can talk about it, the better. But when couples come clean with each other, they're in a much better place. Nobody wants to be lied to about money, especially within a relationship. I've worked with women who are afraid to approach their spouses with conversations about money because they are hiding something or afraid. Sometimes it helps to bring in a neutral third party.

For example, when I'm with a couple, I can support them by answering any questions either may have, and then all three of us can create a solution together. My presence diminishes the stress level between the couple. My advice is for you to say, "I'm sorry for lying to you about X," and be honest about where you want to go from there.

Get real. Be genuine. Admit that you messed up and explain why you've been lying about it. Most of the time, it's not the credit card statement itself that you're avoiding—it's the negative reaction you're expecting from the other person. But when you come clean, you'd be surprised how often a spouse will say, "Well, you should have just told me, and we would've figured something out."

It's not that big of a deal unless you're lying about something major. I once worked with a woman who kept refinancing and refinancing and refinancing a home, and her husband really didn't know much about it, so he trusted his wife to continue doing so. But she knew in the back of her mind that they would never be able to pay off their house. That knowledge was causing her far greater stress. So, my job was to create an exit strategy that supported both of them. I said, "I understand why you did what you did, but now how do we fix this together? By taking these simple steps, both of you are getting involved because you're both equally responsible."

Often, one person will be managing finances poorly while their spouse doesn't want to get involved, leaving all that responsibility to the other person. Both people should play equal roles in the household finances. A third party can help determine how both spouses can get involved financially and support each other, ultimately alleviating the burden. Communication is key. You can't assume that they're aware of the situation when you didn't share.

Teach your children about money.

If you decided to become parents, know that you should be teaching your kids about money. Teach them that when they receive money, they should save some before spending the rest. You know, "Pay yourself first." You can try teaching that at a very young age. Explain the impact of getting money back. You work, you earn money, you keep it, you invest it, you protect yourself. Most importantly, you protect your money.

By having this conversation, you're able to create a legacy and a shift in dynamics when it comes to your family. My mother didn't have that conversation with me, but I was always interested in the topic. My kids will be raised very differently than I was because I was always interested in how money works and I want them to be interested, too.

We work 40, 45 hours a week—sometimes even more—to bring in the money, so we should be able to talk about it and maximize it at the end of the day. The subject shouldn't be swept under the rug. The amount of money that we're bringing in isn't the important part. What matters is how we're spending it, how we're investing it, how we're protecting it, how it's growing for us, and what we're role modeling for our children. So, talk about it.

Keep communication lines and your willingness to compromise open.

Your spouse may have very different ideas about your family's future. You may never know what those ideas are if the two of you don't have frank discussions about your finances on a regular basis. Ultimately, you'll want to fulfill both of your goals, but know that there's got to be a compromise from both sides.

Choosing whether to send your kids to a private school or a public school is an important decision that impacts your finances and should be made by both of you. Another potential question for spouses to ask one another is, "Who is saving up for retirement? Am I going to depend on you for retirement or will we split the responsibility?"

For women who are homemakers, this is a particularly important point of discussion. Obviously, these women are not going to have a retirement plan. Their husbands need to be aware that they can get an IRA for their spouses while they are supporting their family by being stay-at-home moms. Also, even if you don't see eye-to-eye with your spouse about your finances, there will always be certain things you're going to agree on, even if it's something as simple as, "We have to pay the bills on time."

I've noticed that men are usually risk-takers. I know a lot of women who are risk-takers as well, but men are typically more willing to make a big move such as buying a home. Sometimes, a man will buy a home when he's single while a woman might think twice and say, "I'm going to buy a house when I get married."

Communicate with your spouse and let him know what's a deal breaker and what's not. For example, let's say your husband wants a boat, and you know you really can't afford it. You guys need to talk about that. As a compromise, you might say, "Honey, let's go ahead and save for a boat. If we start now, we can go out and buy a boat once we have the full payment." Keep those communication lines open and be ready to compromise every now and then.

CASE STUDY: Money and Marriage

I had a client situation that was horrible. A woman came to me and said, "My husband drinks a lot. He drinks a whole lot." I said, "How much is a whole lot?" She said, "I don't know." I said, "Do you think he knows how much he drinks?" Once again, she said she didn't know. So, I said, "Why don't we find out?" She said, "What do you mean?" I recommended that, for the next three months, she review the bank statements and highlight every single time he spent money at the liquor store. Then, I told her to show the statements and totals to her husband. I told her to approach him out of love, not of out pointing out of that he's doing something wrong. I asked her to just try saying, "Hey honey, I notice that in the last three months, these were the totals from the liquor store. I wanted you to take a look at them. They're about $600."

This is a family that couldn't afford $100 let alone $600 to spend on alcohol. They are financially strapped. By approaching it like that with her husband as opposed to letting it be, or letting it bother her, or nagging him about it, all she did was make him aware. He had no idea he was doing this. Mind you, he's also on automatic.

After becoming aware of it, he started cutting back, little by little. Not immediately, but it took him a little while. So, she kept doing this every few months. "Oh, this is what it was. This is what it was," and she just left it there. Where she started noticing a pattern, he started spending less at the liquor store.

What she was doing, which wasn't any better, was that because she would get upset that he would buy alcohol, she would go out and shop for random things she didn't need. She would be upset and think, "He's doing this, and I don't care. I'm just going to go shopping and spend the same amount of money." I said, "What's the difference between him and you?" She said, "What do you mean?" I said, "Two wrongs don't make a right. What's the difference?"

He had no idea she was doing this, or maybe he did. I said, "Now you're putting even more fuel into the fire, so you're not doing anything better. How are you solving this problem?" She said she didn't know. I said, "Let me ask you something, you have a fine little hustle going on. You do pastries." I said, "If I were to ask you how much money you have made from that, what would your answer be?" She said she didn't know. I said, "So you're operating from the same awareness. Why don't you become the force of saying, 'I'm going to be responsible for me. I'm going to have, I'm going to provide, I'm going to run my business like a business. I'm going to keep that money aside, and I'm going to let him know.' Then when you're aware of your money, you can say to your husband, 'Hey we're short on money this time. This is what we need.'"

She decided to start communicating in this different realm instead of pointing the finger at him. So, she did this for about a year. They ended up saving enough money to go on a little weekend getaway with the entire family. She's got three kids. She and her husband paid cash, and they went to Big Bear. They had never done that before.

Chapter Nine

SETTING UP YOUR BUSINESS FOR SUCCESS

Always start with your why.

Simon Sinek is a mentor who has no idea he's my mentor. He advises business owners to start with their why. Why are you in business? Why do you want to do this? A good way to do this is by writing your mission statement.

My why is my parents. If I hadn't paid attention to where they were in their life together, where they were at in retirement, where they were at financially…and just really examining the history of our family finances, I would never have created my company. My why has kept be going every business day. My mission of creating awareness about easy, sustainable, and responsible financial planning propels me every step of the way.

When clients ask me to evaluate their finances and provide other options, I always ask why. Why are you here? What do you want to accomplish? Why do you want it accomplished? Why do you want your kids to go to college? Our relationship starts with their why as well.

In the Latin community, in the city where I live, in my family, and even with many friends who are entrepreneurs,

I've noticed that we are all lacking the guidance we need to start and run a successful business. We want our own business, and we're willing to do whatever it takes. However, we don't have the structure behind it. My purpose for writing this chapter is to raise the awareness that, when you become a business owner, you become 100% responsible for all business roles as well as your employees.

It's not simply opening a business because you're passionate about something, such as being a chef, and making that a part of your personal income and accounts. When you open a business, you must take responsibility for everything, including your health benefits, business taxes, employee payroll, and more. Not only are you a chef, but you're a chef who must run a business!

There are many small businesses in the Latin market, but a lot of business owners don't have the guidance of, "what's next?" Latinos and Latinas have an amazing work ethic. It's part of our culture. But just working hard doesn't necessarily lead to business or family success. Amazing businesses are going out of business all the time because the business owners focused on doing the business and forgot to run their business.

I have a client who is a phenomenal trainer. She trains her pregnant mommies and then guides them through the process of post-partum. However, even though she's a business owner, she doesn't have a business owner mentality. When it comes to the business mindset, she freaks out. She's asks me questions like, "Why do I have to ask for business?

Why do I need separate accounts?" My answer is simple. "Because you're running a business; to keep your business going and growing, you must market your business and continue to grow your client base."

When I met with another client and asked her about her business expenses and accounts (just like I do with personal clients), she gave it to me all mixed in with her personal finances. As a business owner, you must know what goes in and out in both, and you must create a budget within both. She didn't realize she needed to separate her business expenses from her personal expenses.

Does this sound like you? It sounded like me as I began to learn about running my business.

When I first started in business, I didn't set up my corporation immediately because I had no money. I was running my business out of my home office. I didn't really need a real office yet, but because I thought that was important, I got myself into a lease that I could barely afford. But I wanted to have an office, because that's what real business people do.

From my experience, I thought I was just going to meet with clients, help them with their financial planning, and that was that. That was my main focus. I thought that's all there was to it. But then I learned more about what it really takes, and I focused more on marketing and the creative side of my business. I asked myself important questions, like: How can I be creative to get out there and be on the media or the news? How can I put myself out there in that realm? How can I let women know I have a valuable service to provide? Who do I need to help me? So, I really started wearing all the hats, and then I started meeting with my clients, and then I started to work with important partners to grow my business.

When I started my business, which was nine years ago, I said I'm going to give it five years to see if this works. So, I was already doubting myself from the jump, instead of saying I'm all in, I'm focused, and this is what I need to do to become successful. Then I realized that as long as every single year I was doing something to better my business, I would expand and prosper. When it came time to build my website, it was a year I couldn't afford professional pictures. The ones I wanted were about $1,200. When you're starting a business, you have a tendency to go for what's the cheapest. But I didn't see it that way. I saved the money to say, "No I want that particular thing, because that is going to be my image."

I had to transform myself year by year by year about my business. I had to transform my mental thoughts about where I was, where I started, where I'm headed, and what's next.

So, I started paying attention to the bigger brands.

There's a supermarket in California run by a local family from very humble beginnings. They have an empire of grocery stores now called Northgate Gonzalez Market. They just built the newest, hottest, super amazing store. I love walking in there. Everything's new and fresh and organic, and it's beautiful in there. It makes you want to shop for quality food, and they came from nothing.

This is not the Dad's business…this is the family business. Everybody plays a role. They also were strategic in that their business is about building relationships. They've sponsored events, they've donated $10,000 scholarships, and so much more, but they don't want publicity for doing so.

I thought, "Why would somebody not want to know that Northgate Gonzalez Market just donated a $10,000 scholarship for marketing purposes?" Jimmy Gonzalez says it's because "We're not in the business of just giving money. We're in the business of having people know who we are and our products that we provide. Not for them to ask us for money." I was like, "Oh, wow." They're very solid about their mission.

Jimmy also says, "I don't run a business, I am the business." I asked, "What do you mean I don't run a business, I am the business?" His business is what he's about. He embodies the entire mission for his markets. So, it's like if you're hiring me, you're hiring me for who I am, which is the business. It just happens to be that I'm in business.

To me that was powerful. I was so excited and said to him, "Oh my God, Jimmy, you know what that gave me? It gave me clarity to get out of my own way. It gave me clarity and focus to understand that I am what I was creating. My business happens to have my name and face all over it, but it has nothing to do with me. It's about my business...of awareness, of perspective, of creating wealth in a completely different level. It just happens to be wrapped up in a business called Eva Macias & Associates." So, Once I was 100% clear on my vision and embodying my brand, it was no longer, "Oh let me sell another plan."

It was about, "Let me create awareness, and the plan will sell itself."

I think when we let go of the expectation of the numbers of what it's supposed to look like, and we understand the impact and what that's creating toward others, before you know it, the receiving starts coming in ways that you're like, "What did I do, what happened here?"

After nine years in business, I have heard one form or another of the lessons below. I hope they help you.

Learn from the masters.

Pay attention to the bigger brands, and you can learn a lot. For example, after I saw the documentary about McDonalds, it is what started shaping my business when I heard one of the gentlemen say, "In every state that you go, you will always see an American flag and the golden arches. We will have our golden arch be seen just like that." To me, that was a powerful "wow" moment. I could picture that golden M in the arch. And then I could imagine my logo as an E, and if that E was in every single place…wow. It was an inspirational moment for me.

Another thing you can learn from the masters is recognizing that McDonalds is not in the business of hamburgers. We think they are, but they're not. They're in the business of real estate. That was another eye-opener as a business owner. Because I had been thinking, "Oh, I'm in the financial planning business, and I talk to people about retirement. I talk to people about life insurance and the different benefits and how to read their benefits and so on." Then I realized, "Wait a minute, that's what I do, but I'm in the business of creating awareness. I'm in the business of extending a mindset. I'm in the business of that. I just happen to do financial planning."

Set up a corporation.

There are many reasons why it's important to set up a corporation. The first reason is that you get to have an entity that is your company. A lot of women who are business owners haven't taken ownership of it. What if, over time, you want to sell your company? Or, you may just want to get paid from your company.

It's also important, for tax purposes, to start a corporation. What your corporation does and the amount of income you make are two different things. You may pay yourself a salary from your corporation. You may not. You may take it at the end of the year. Or you may just take one lump-sum withdrawal.

When setting up your corporation, you should also be keeping your business as real as possible. Tax brackets are very different when it comes to business tax versus personal tax. Personal tax is actually much higher than business tax. If you were to set yourself up with a corporation, you might end up paying fewer taxes.

Take some time to consider your options. I know a lot of women with businesses who are running them out of their homes, but they haven't set their businesses up in the way that will ultimately support their finances.

Understand your business taxes.

Taxes, like death, are a certainty in life. Like how we know that death is inevitable, we also know that we must pay taxes. And at the end of the day, it doesn't matter whether you pay your taxes now or later. You're going to need to pay them at some point. So, play by the rules from the beginning.

When it comes to taxes, know whether you're paying on an individual basis or if you're in a corporation. Know how the rules are going to apply to you on a personal basis and on a corporate basis. And, like I said, pay your taxes. The sooner you pay your taxes, the better. You could end up with a levy on your bank account. Who wants that because you're not paying your taxes? I'm a big believer of paying your taxes first. This way everything else that you're currently doing will set you up to win.

Know the three most important people you need to solidify your business.

A business tip that I received in starting my business is that the three key people that you need to build a solid relationship with are your CPA, your attorney, and your bookkeeper. They're your new best friends. You can ask them anything without being afraid that it's a stupid question. Use other people as tools to enhance your business and set a solid foundation.

Network in a way that supports your business.

It's important to understand the networking behind your business. You also need to network in a way that supports your business. There are numbers of networking events that happen every day, but are they representative of the mission of your business? In the beginning, I wasted a lot of my time because I thought, "Oh, I'll just network over there. Or show up over here." I never knew who I would meet, because I didn't have a clear focus of what I wanted my business to be. Identify where your business model falls and attend only those events that further your mission.

Be consistent with your marketing and messaging.

One of the things that I feel Latin people don't do with their business is marketing. They don't spend on marketing. They know a good portion of their profits goes to salaries, but they rarely re-invest a portion of their profits into marketing. It's word of mouth. That's how they get started, or that's how they maintain business. Then they're comfortable, they make a decent living, and then they die. I mean it sounds horrible, but really that's what it is.

In my business, I've been consistent with the marketing behind it. I've been consistent with posting on Facebook. And because I've been consistent in people's eyes, they see me as a credible source. They know that I'm very involved. They know that I'm not just in this for the short term, I'm in this for the long haul.

But it wasn't like that at first. I resisted social media. I thought that was merely a social thing. When people told me that Facebook is the new marketing, I didn't know what they meant.

But I knew I needed to expand myself within technology while keeping my business simple at the same time. In and out simple. I've made it easy by learning it and remaining consistent. I hear from people all the time, "Oh I trust her, she's been in business." Oftentimes, by Facebook Business Page members recognize me on the street and say hi. It's a great feeling.

Use your own money like a bank.

I've worked with women who have $150,000 in their account to borrow from, and yet they are living with $25,000 in credit card debts. Every single month, they're stressed out about how they're going to make ends meet. Setting up your business is one thing, but using your own money as a business can ultimately be a beautiful thing.

So, this woman has $150,000, and she owes $25,000. She owes different creditors, she owes credit card companies, and on top of that she's paying high interest rates. What if she decided to borrow her own money, like she would from a bank, to pay off all these creditors and credit card debts? Then, every time she makes a payment, she's paying back interest on her own money. We may not like banks, but they have the system down. You borrow money from them, and they charge you a really high interest rate.

If you have both money and debt, figure out a system of checks and balances where you can use your own money to support you. You will get out of debt much more quickly and potentially reduce the interest rate of what you're paying.

Let's say you normally have your accounts in a 401k, and if you're borrowing a loan from that, then your paycheck through your salary deduction is automatically paying that debt.

This allows us to shift our minds from, "Oh, I have this money and I have this debt," to "How can I use my own money to support my financial future in my business?" You can apply this concept to your personal finances as well, but it works especially well if you own a business. Now is the time to start thinking like a business owner.

Decide if you want a business partner.

Make sure you know if you want to be in a partnership or not. What's more important to you...driving solo or creating a collaboration? If you do want a partnership, be crystal clear about the expectations of each partner and have it put in writing. That way, you won't be any wishy-washy, oh we were supposed to get this, now this, or this. Partnerships are just like marriages. It's constant communication and constant conversation. I talk to my business partner as much as I talk to my husband.

Protect your business partner's life.

Many times, when there are business partnerships, owners don't consider that the death of their business partner will impact their business. But it will! Not only on the business side, but also with the surviving spouse. Based on the clients I've worked with, it's rare when one business owner out of 20 in a meeting says, "Oh yeah, I am protected against everything. If my business partner were to die that is his or her loss, but the business can still run. Their spouse is not going to take 50% of that business." You can't rely on platitudes or verbal agreements. With a two-person insurance policy, it will pay the business, the financial loss of that particular person, and it will pay out the spouse. That way, everyone is taken care of.

An amazing insurance called Key Person Life Insurance exists and will actually allow you to protect your business. In a partnership, both parties are key elements in making sure that the business is running successfully or in making sure that the business is profitable. Let's just say you happen to be the brains behind the business while your partner is the one who handles the marketing. Both of you need each other to keep this business running.

It's important that you protect your partner's life because your business and life will be affected. If your partner were to die, how would it impact you? How can you make sure that you're both protected, your families are protected, and your business is protected, so that there's never a misunderstanding in case tragedy strikes and one of you were to pass?

So, yes...protect your assets. When dealing with a business, take a look into Key Person Life Insurances. There is more to it than just an insurance policy with a 30-year term. It's more about making sure that your business is set up solidly.

Pass your business to your children.

With family businesses, I've known parents who have had the businesses forever, and they started it from the ground up. Now they're ready to retire, but in the back of their minds, they keep thinking, "No, I'm the only one who can do this."

By educating your kids about how to run a business, your legacy can continue when you pass. I have seen multimillion-dollar businesses go down the drain after a death in the family because the parents in charge never taught their children how to run it.

Initiate a conversation with your family and your offspring. When you're talking about finances in the business, get them involved. When you're making big decisions—even if their opinions or feedback won't be used—make sure they're around to see how you handle the business. Because, at one point, you may need to leave your own business because of health reasons or old age. What's going to happen then?

You will need to hand the reins over to someone else. Don't put that extra stress on yourself when you can start teaching your kids and your family how to continue running that business, so it remains successful and a family legacy.

Teach your kids the core values of your business.

The generation gap can be large, so it's important that your children understand where you're coming from. Familiarize them with your mission statement and explain why you have it. No matter what generation you're a part of, values are still values at the end of the day. When your kids know the mission statement behind your business and understand why that's so important, the business is much more profitable. Everyone is on the same page.

I often hear my clients say things like, "Well, my son wants me to promote this on social media, and I know nothing about social media." These questions usually occur during conversations about how to expand your business. If you are of the younger generation, what if your parents aren't too crazy about social media? Well then, maybe you can help run this aspect of the business. Have discussions about how social media will impact your business. What are some of the returns that you want to see? How much are you investing in sales and marketing when you add social media to the mix?

There is a saying: "A family that eats together, stays together." Or similarly, "A family that prays together, stays together." Likewise, a family that discusses core values regarding money will ultimately have similar visions for the business. The business will be much easier to keep together. But your child may still bring a fresh outlook and say, "I understand you want me to run the business this way. But now I'm showing you a new way of doing business that will still fit within your core values: trust, respect, client satisfaction." Conversations like these are invaluable.

So, teach your kids those core values that enhance your business. If you're not available, and the clients are dealing with your kids, you want your kids to be knowledgeable and not rude. You don't want to lose a potential customer. This is your responsibility, not only as a parent, but also as a boss. You're playing two key roles.

Stretch your dollars when starting a business.

Always know how much of your own personal money you're bringing into the business, whether it's a startup or a business you're applying income to. I have seen family businesses that have gone bad because one of the spouses wanted to keep it while the other one didn't.

Set a budget for your business and say, "We're not going to expand any more than this. Whatever that decided amount is, we're going to run a successful business out of it." It's very important that you agree, from the beginning, to set a specific budget within all of the different key factors of your business: leases, marketing, company cars, etc. Don't stray from those set amounts and those boundaries you create.

In the beginning, even if you're running a profitable business alone, start treating it as if you were a really big company. By setting up that foundation, over time it will get bigger and expand, if that's what you want it to do. And if it doesn't expand, I'm sure you may want to sell it at some point.

Stretch your dollars now by setting a budget. This will make it much easier for you to detach yourself from it later, whether it's because you no longer want the business or because you're ready to retire.

Stay balanced between running your business and spending time with your family.

Don't bring work home. Business is for work, and family time is for family. Sometimes, all families will talk about at home is business, so much so that they forget about all the other things that matter in life. They forget to have real conversations: "How are you doing, how are you feeling, what's going on? Tell me what's going on with you as a person, not with all of the things you're doing with your business."

If you want a profitable business, you need to figure out that balance. For example, if you work 9 to 5 in your own business, then work from 9 to 5 and come home for dinner and leave all that behind until the next morning. These are the key elements that will ultimately give you a balanced life.

Even people who are very important—not only to their family but also to society—still go home at 5 o'clock. Their impact on society is huge. They're running a multimillion-dollar corporation, and they still make sure to get home for dinner more often than not. At the end of day, you may have a very profitable business, but if your family life stinks, your kids won't want to be part of it.

I met a man who ran his business extremely well. All he did was work. That's all he knew how to do. He didn't know how to have a relationship with his wife. He didn't know how to have a relationship with his kids. And when I asked those kids if they were excited to inherit their father's business, they said, "No, because I don't want to end up like Dad."

Compromise and communication are very important. Balance out your life, because while the most important thing may be having the money to provide for your family, it all means nothing if you no longer have a strong family unit to provide for.

Review your financial plan before investing more in your business.

Pay attention to any red flags when you review your financial plan. I have known people who wanted to continue running their business even though they hadn't seen any profit for 10 years. If you look at your financial plan and realize it hasn't been a profitable business, learn how to let go. This may not be the business for you. By doing financial reviews with your business partners, with your associates, and with your spouse, you'll keep yourself in check. You'll know whether you're making a profit, and if you're not, you can pinpoint the reason why it's not happening.

You may need to invest in other departments, but know your budget. It's crucial to look at your financial plan. There are restaurants out there today that are running on negative accounts. How can you provide a service if you're in the hole $200,000? How can you, as an owner, provide customers the experience and ambience of an excellent, exquisite meal when the servers are silently thinking, "We may not even have a job tomorrow because the boss is struggling so much financially."

Get a review from someone who's not emotionally attached to the business. Talking to a neutral third party, normally a financial coach, will bring to light any blind spots that you can't see yourself. They can help support you and what you're creating for your business.

Know the benefit plans available to you as a business owner.

You may just be starting up your company. There may be no one else involved right now…no partners or employees. Even so, you can provide benefits—like a life insurance policy— for yourself. You can still qualify for that. On the other hand, if you have 10 people working at your company, you can look into offering group insurance.

If you haven't had the opportunity to set up a 401k, you can always refer to Roth IRAs. You can always put money in a cash-value life insurance. It doesn't matter whether you're a business owner or you're just part of the family. Pay yourself first.

Often, if you're not running a successful business, your money is going out all the time. Even if money is coming in, you may not be paying attention to it and what you're paying out. Because this is part of the business, you must pay attention to your finances, you must pay yourself first, and you also must pay out to others as well.

Avoid start-up costs.

Frequently, there are no startup costs for life insurance plans and IRAs, whether they are traditional or Roth IRAs. If you do happen to set up a 401k, there will be a sign-up cost, which is usually paid to a third-party administrator. These people are administering your retirement plan and making sure that everything is being properly done through salary reduction.

Figure out what resources you can provide for yourself and for your employees at the lowest cost to you. This is part of doing your homework. In the future, once your company gets much bigger and you choose to set up 401k plans, there will be a cost. That cost varies from situation to situation. You will sit down with the third-party administrator and determine those costs. But at the end of the day, you can definitely get the right benefits without paying a dime other than your monthly investment. In other words, there are ways to avoid start-up costs. A financial expert can tell you more.

CONCLUSION

The price you pay for not paying attention
is very expensive.

On a visit to Bulletproof Labs in Santa Monica, I stepped into a virtual tank that had no water and was immediately deprived of my senses. Instantly, I went into this meditative state where I thought I was walking on clouds. I was weightless and felt like I could fly. It was a 20-minute experience where I was alert and wide awake. I was able to get in tune with the cellular level of my body as well as alter the way my brain and body functioned.

Pretty powerful stuff.

And then I stepped out, gathered my belongings, went to the front desk to pay, and headed out the door. I automatically walked to my car, slid in, turned the key, and took off for wherever I was going.

What had just happened to me? I took a moment to slow down my fast-paced thoughts and behavior and pay attention to the fast-paced world all around me that I had so easily become a part of again. As I drove down Main Street, I watched the people who were walking down the street instead. I wondered if their pace allowed them to pay attention to their thoughts. I recognized that the pace of my life meant that I only allowed myself to shut down because I paid for 20 minutes to put myself in a machine where I could be with myself and only myself and my brain and my thoughts. And as soon as the 20 minutes were over, I went back to my automatic way of being. And that way was not paying attention. This was the first time it hit me…I wasn't walking my talk about paying attention. I realized it wasn't just about money, it also had to be about paying attention to the surroundings and life all around you.

Earlier today I was craving a cheeseburger, and I thought, "Why? Am I bored? Am I hungry? Or am I just jonesing for a cheeseburger? What's coming up for me?" These are questions I ask myself all the time now as I learn to process things and understand why I'm wanting to take a certain action or do a certain behavior. I now make sure to pay attention to see if I want to create a different result.

Of course, the same thing applies when it comes to your finances. Take a moment to stop and ask yourself, "Why am I doing this? Is it supporting my goals and values or is it not?" So, if money is a result of the consistency of our actions over time, let's pay attention to the whole formula. When a friend or a client says, "I want money! I want money!" I'm like, okay then…let's talk about your actions. Let's talk about your mindset. Let's talk about where you've been and where you can go, and *then* we'll talk about money.

The same holds true for you. What result do you want to create? What life do you want to live? What is your why?

I saw a post on Facebook while writing this book that said to make sure you "Count your ROI." The post drew my attention because knowing that "return on investment" is something I practice in providing financial services. But what's your return on investment when you spend thousands of hours in a business that you don't know will work? You don't know that. Neither do I. So, to pretend to say I know the ROI on everything just because I'm a financial expert is bullshit.

I don't know what the ROI of this book is going to be. I don't. Why? Because I don't know how big it can get or the impact it could have. I'm not going to limit myself by thinking, "Oh, the ROI on this must be this or it's not worth the effort." Because again, I'm not writing it for the ROI. I'm writing it for the awareness. How do you project ROI on awareness?

With that in mind, as I close this book, I want you to remain aware of these three final reminders.

Persist and you will succeed.

If you are persistent and realistic with your financial goals, you will get where you want to be. Before you know it, you'll be thinking, "Wow! It's not that difficult to put $300 away. I was just making it harder than it needed to be." If it gets a bit tough along the way, don't give up. Adjust your budget to do what's best for you, such as not going out for a month or giving fewer presents during the holidays. Don't beat yourself up. You're setting an example for other people, particularly your children, when you persevere in the face of adversity.

Be consistent.

You've read this many times by now. No matter what happens, make sure you're always protecting your money and always paying attention to your money. Create your budget each and every month. Reformulate your financial plan and your plan of action to maintain your results. Be consistent with your smart financial habits. Your steady commitment will pay off...big time.

Pay attention.

When you create the time to pay attention to your financial plan, you will experience the results you want to achieve. Once you do, you can experience even more abundance to create the freedom and the free time to spend with those who matter the most...*your family!* This is your time to stop, reflect, and take action. You owe it to yourself and the ones you love.

Got 60 minutes? Then you've got plenty of time to visit www.EvaMacias.com/60min and get going on creating your financial plan for the future.

Made in the USA
San Bernardino, CA
22 February 2018